CANYONEERING

HOW TO EXPLORE THE CANYONS
OF THE GREAT SOUTHWEST

D0872583

0 11557 02700 6

Also by
JOHN ANNERINO

PHOTO ESSAY

APACHE
The Sacred Path to Womanhood

PEOPLE OF LEGEND
Native Americans of the Southwest

THE WILD COUNTRY OF MEXICO
La tierra salvaje de México

CANYONS OF THE SOUTHWEST
The Great Canyon Country from Colorado to Northern Mexico

HIGH RISK PHOTOGRAPHY
The Adventure Behind the Image

WILDERNESS TRAVEL

HIKING THE GRAND CANYON

ADVENTURING IN ARIZONA

NONFICTION

RUNNING WILD
An Extraordinary Adventure of the Human Spirit

DEAD IN THEIR TRACKS
Crossing America's Borderlands

CANYONEERING

HOW TO EXPLORE THE CANYONS
OF THE GREAT SOUTHWEST

JOHN ANNERINO

STACKPOLE
BOOKS

Published by
STACKPOLE BOOKS
5067 Ritter Road
Mechanicsburg, PA 17055
www.stackpolebooks.com

Printed in the United States of America

10 9 8 7 6 5 4 3 2 1

FIRST EDITION

Front cover photograph and design by John Annerino
Back cover photograph by Chris Keith
All photographs by John Annerino, unless otherwise noted

Library of Congress Cataloging-in-Publication Data

Annerino, John.
    Canyoneering: how to explore the canyons of the Great Southwest/John Annerino.—1st ed.
       p.   cm.
    Includes bibliographical references (p. 139) and index.
    ISBN 0-8117-2700-9
    1. Canyons—Southwest, New—Guidebooks. I. Title.
GB566.S68A54   1999
796.51′0979′09144—dc21   98-43089
                                                      CIP

CONTENTS

For my love, Alejandrina, who has helped me forge a path of happiness and fulfillment in life, and to my son, who I hope will blaze his own.

ACKNOWLEDGMENTS

Thanks to those friends and canyoneers who accompanied me on my most memorable canyon adventures—and to the climbers, boatmen and -women, and the indigenous canyon dwellers like the Guarijío and Tarahumara who opened my eyes to the broad view of canyoneering: Michael St. Clair, Suzanne Jordan, Martha Clark, Robb Elliott, Louise Teal, Dave Ganci, George Bain, Jason Lohman, Tim Ganey, Craig Hudson, Chris Keith, Chris May, Tony Mangine, Casey Mangine, Rich Nebeker, Bob Farrell, Cilia McClung, and Bill Broyles. I'd also like to thank Linda Lotz, Dave Richwine, and Mark Allison at Stackpole Books.

INTRODUCTION

CANYON DREAMS

I have not been there, but Colca Canyon in Peru is said to be the earth's deepest terrestrial canyon at -14,339 feet; nor have I been to Idaho and Oregon's Hells Canyon, which has been called the deepest canyon in North America at -7,900 feet. So I can only muse on whether they're truly the deepest canyons on their respective continents, as I've come to understand the word *canyon*, or whether they're the deepest mountain gorges. They are not included in this study of canyoneering, because I do not write about what I haven't personally researched and experienced. What I do discuss are the canyons I've studied and explored by foot, raft, rope, canoe, saddle, and camera. They are the canyons of the Great Southwest—a vast and mythic region that encompasses the southwestern United States and northwestern Mexico. It forms the heart of the most spectacular and rugged canyon country in North America, and it includes some of the largest, deepest, and narrowest canyons in the world. It was in the sublime depths of this stony domain that ancient canyon dwellers, explorers, surveyors, and river runners helped define the modern concept of canyoneering. And it was from this canyon realm that I gleaned lessons and perspectives that shaped my own concepts of canyoneering.

My introduction to canyon country took place in my early teens; stifled by the din of a Sun Belt boomtown and the brick walls of my small backyard, I hitchhiked from my parents' house in east Phoenix one weekend to explore Peralta Canyon. It was the legendary portal to central Arizona's Superstition Mountains. The ancestral land of the Pima, Kewevkapaya Yavapai, and Southern Tonto band of Western Apache, the Superstitions had become infamous for tales of Spanish gold, Apache raids, generations of wild-eyed pistol-toting prospectors hypnotized by the myth of the Lost Dutchman's gold, and more than fifty sinister deaths and murders. For a boy and his dog—and the throngs of city dwellers who continue to venture into the mountains' storied reaches—there was no more magical and mysterious place.

A rough-hewn Sonoran Desert mountain range, its maze of canyons and looming pillars of stone characterized what some lost hikers called the Superstitions' "look-alike" interior, and I never tired of exploring it. Nor did I grow bored with the rugged trails, bushwhacks, and scrambles that marked my days; the campfires, canopy of stars, and howling coyotes that soothed my nights. The Superstitions remained my haunt and defined my concepts of both desert survival and canyoneering until I signed on as a boatman one summer to row the Green and Yampa Rivers in Dinosaur National Monument on the Utah-Colorado border.

The ancestral land of the Ute, the canyons of the Green and Yampa Rivers opened up a new world for me as I rowed an army-surplus raft through Browns Park, Gates of Lodore, Disaster Falls, Hell's Half-Mile, and Whirlpool Canyon. This, too, was historic canyon country, the domain of Butch Cassidy's Wild Bunch, hired gun Tom Horn, one-armed explorer Major John Wesley Powell, and pioneer river runners Buzz and Alton Hatch. It was here that I first felt the raw power of white water as my oaken oars were wrenched from my blistered hands, where I first became mesmerized by the oxidized black tapestry of Tiger Wall, where I learned to explore canyon country by running on foot as the Yampa Ute once had done.

From the boneyard of dinosaur remains at the mouth of Split Mountain Canyon, the Green River meanders west-southwest toward Canyonlands National Park, and so did my canyon dreams at summer's end. A year later, I got my chance to row Cataract Canyon; it was Canyonlands' most fearsome stretch of white water and the last undammed stretch of the Colorado River before it boiled into a 186-mile-long pool of water that buried Glen Canyon and created Lake Powell. With a season of river running under my rowing seat and the threat of Mile Long Rapids behind me, I stared at the

During a twelve-day Grand Canyon river trip, boatwoman Louise Teal rows Crystal Rapid at Mile 98 on the Colorado River.

maelstrom of water surging through Big Drop Rapids at 53,000 cubic feet per second (cfs), confident that the exploding haystacks of brown water and V-waves were no match for my skills or wits.

I can't clearly recall at what moment I flipped, when everything turned cold, black, and wet and I was helplessly dragged down to the bottom of the river to meet what some Grand Canyon boatmen call the "green slime." But when I finally breached for air, I popped up alongside my overturned boat hacking up bile, mucus, brown water, and arrogance. I was finally baptized in the great river. In the words of head boatman Mike St. Clair: "There are two kinds of boatmen: those who have flipped, and those who *will*."

I needed to go back to square one. Trying to muscle a baloney boat overloaded with commercial passengers, duffel, and beer was one thing; learning to read the river, what the current was actually doing, and using it was another. A year later, I followed my dreams downstream from Cataract Canyon into the classroom of the Grand Canyon, the ancestral realm of the Southern Paiute, Havasupai, Hualapai, Hopi, and Navajo. It was here that a woman taught me how to read a river that killed thirty men before Bessy Hyde murdered her husband (some think) and became the first woman to run the Colorado River through Cataract and Grand Canyons during the somber days of 1928. My teacher's name was Suzanne Jordan; to the delight of her passengers and the chagrin of other skilled boatwomen who had broken the male mold of bronze river gods boldly rowing through chasms no woman dare enter, Suzanne and her circle of boatwomen called one another "hags." But Suzanne and her crew were anything but tattooed, bar-brawling, beer-swilling louts. A beautiful, red-haired woman from Alabama, Suzanne spent a month of her life, on two consecutive twelve-day paddle trips down the Colorado River, showing me something in the river that I couldn't see for myself when I first drifted into Marble Canyon as the paddle captain of an 18-foot Avon Spirit carrying five anxious paddlers.

"Just sit here with me and watch the river," Suzanne would tell me as we scouted House Rock Rapid, Crystal, or the bubble line in Lava. Mesmerized by her velvety southern voice, I stared at the river and, at first, saw only the slick current pouring into another Colorado River pool-drop rapid, blind to the nuances of the current. And Suzanne would say, "Look what the current's doing there. See how it's piling against that rock." And I'd look, and if I still couldn't see the current from the river, Suzanne would fling a piece of driftwood into the torrent and I'd watch it get hammered against a boulder or sucked into a ledge hole. She would say, "You don't want to be there." Then she would ask, "Where are you going to go?" And I'd use my stick to draw a line in the sand showing what I thought was the best run through the big water, and she would say, "Watch it. See what the current's doing there?" I'd nod. Then, before I got back into my boat and recinched my life jacket to harness the butterflies in my stomach, she would add, "Never get locked into a certain run. You can't always see what the current's doing. And you might not be where you thought you'd be."

For years, I was locked into the Grand Canyon; it consumed my life because it was the only place I thought I wanted to be. And as I began racking up the river miles, I repeatedly learned that the maxim was true: "You never go down the same river twice." I was

lost in the maze of canyons, adventures, discoveries, and friend-
ships that unfolded with each new river trip; that is, until one
morning I woke up with sand and dew on my face and realized that
I'd made twenty trips down the Grand. It was not a large number
in comparison with the hundred or more trips of some boatmen
and -women. But my tenure as a Grand Canyon boatman opened
up new worlds to me, and it redefined my concept of canyoneering.
Was canyoneering captaining a 12-foot Redshank paddle raft
through Lava Falls at 33,000 cfs without flipping? Was it walking
out the South Kaibab Trail at high noon during the blistering heat
of summer to search for a lost foreign diplomat? Was it rappelling
into the frigid narrows of Deer Creek Falls with thinly clad boatwomen? Was it spelunking into subterranean caves behind the
Grand Canyon's tumultuous cascades? Was it swimming into the
Blue Room, an underwater cave, on a single breath of air without
panicking? Was it cliff jumping off Beaver Falls? Was it scrambling
up Nautiloid Canyon on a short river hike for a geology talk? Was it
being rocked asleep each night by the Colorado River as I lay on my
bobbing raft, my dreams lost among the Milky Way and shooting
stars? Canyoneering had come to define each of those moments for
me, though river runners—including myself—rarely used its modern appellation to describe such experiences.

Canyoneering had also come to mean climbing the Grand
Canyon's monolithic sandstone temples. At one end of the spec-
trum, that might entail scrambling in the footsteps of the Anasazi
up 7,646-foot Shiva Temple; at the other end, it meant making the
first ascent of, say, the Southwest Face of 7,123-foot Zoroaster Temple with veteran canyon rock climbers Dave Ganci and George
Bain. Like river running, climbing in the Grand Canyon required its
own unique combination of canyoneering skills: the ability to make
arduous descents and re-ascents; keen route finding; the ability to
cross exposed and precipitous terrain unroped; an intimate knowledge of the inner Canyon's marginal water sources and geology;
safety skills; endurance; and, if the objective involved more than
scrambling, a proficiency in rock climbing on crumbly limestone
and sandstone. Like the myriad activities one associates with Grand
Canyon river running, climbing in this great inverted mountain

range was not called canyoneering, either. Nobody ever called me up and said, "Let's go canyoneering this weekend." It was: "You wanna do Buddha?" (Do you want to climb Buddha Temple?)

Canyoneering had also come to define the five-year period in my life I spent training for, and embarking on, three multiday distance runs through the heart of the Grand Canyon. I was intent on proving my hypothesis that ancient canyon dwellers ran through the inner Canyon long before the first Spaniards, prospectors, and river runners ventured into it, and the only way to do that was to trace out and run the ancient canyon paths myself. In 1980, there was a six-day, 170-mile run below the South Rim; in 1981, a seven-day, 210-mile run along the ancient Hopi-Havasupai trade route atop the South Rim; and in 1982, an eight-and-a-half-day, 250-mile run below the seldom-explored North Rim. Throughout these fleet-footed journeys, I continually pushed myself to the limits of physical and mental endurance in order to reach the canyon horizon line alive; and in doing so, I once again redefined my concept of canyoneering. Was canyoneering running alone along hanging terraces and narrow ledges, far removed from the outside world and with only the remotest chance of rescue if I made a mistake? Was it shivering all night around a bivouac fire without a sleeping bag? Was it cliff climbing without ropes? Was it swimming flood-swept torrents? Was it going without food? Was it nearly dying of thirst?

Canyoneering meant all those things to me, too; it also defined the base knowledge and experiences that led up to that spirit quest, as well as subsequent adventures that took me to the far reaches of canyon country: Canyoneering meant entering the granite depths of California's Sierra Nevada, carrying rafts on packhorses, to run the treacherous Forks of the Kern River. It was photographing the trials and tribulations of an Executive Outward group for a national magazine as Fortune 500 CEOs canoed and explored the border canyons of Big Bend National Park. It was boulder-hopping up Cañon del Diablo (Canyon of the Devil) to climb the 10,154-foot summit of northern Baja's Picacho del Diablo. It was using my cameras to document the traditional ceremonies and lifeways of the Yaqui, Guarijío, Mountain Pima, and Tarahumara in the foothills,

The author on a perilous Tyrolean rope traverse below Thunder River Falls, North Rim of the Grand Canyon.

PHOTO FROM THE JOHN ANNERINO COLLECTION

canyons, and mesas of Mexico's Sierra Madre Occidental. It was trekking alone down the length of the Little Colorado River Gorge. It was swimming the plunge pools of Wet Beaver Creek with friends, playing in the quicksand of Paria Narrows, crossing the frothing cataract of Thunder River on a Tyrolean rope traverse, and being swept away by my first river romance. To me, elements of canyoneering also defined each of those experiences—and the sum of them. Like river running, climbing, and distance running in the Grand Canyon, however, these experiences were rarely referred to as canyoneering by other practitioners—though each required its own blend of canyoneering skills. After two decades of exploring the mountains, deserts, and canyons of the Great Southwest, canyoneering came to mean the place, one's knowledge of it, and the experience; it was more than a simplistic view of a specific activity.

Many names continue to sing in my imagination whenever I dream of exploring the world beneath the horizon line. There is Matkatamiba, Chaco, Satevó, the Little C, the Río de Piaxtla, and many other canyons lost to the modern world, the rush of humanity, and the black hole of cyberspace. They, too, merit exploration, preservation, and respect, whether you take the broad view of canyoneering as exploring canyon country by hiking, trekking, distance running, river running, climbing, photographing, and studying its cultural fabric and geography, or the narrow view that canyoneering only means swimming, floating, and rappelling slot canyons. While the flavor of the Great Southwest will be unmistakable throughout the following pages, I hope that this book proves valuable to you however you define canyoneering and wherever your own canyon dreams lead you.

Noonday rest in Marble Canyon
JOHN WESLEY POWELL

OVERVIEW
Canyon Country of the
Great Southwest

1. Zion National Park
2. Escalante/Grand Staircase
   National Monument
3. Canyonlands/Arches
   National Park
4. Black Canyon of the Gunnison
5. Buckskin Gulch/Paria Canyon
6. Glen Canyon National
   Recreation Area
7. Grand Canyon National Park
8. Canyons of the Mogollon Rim
9. Cañon del Diablo
10. Canyons of Tiburón Island
11. Barrancas of the Sierra
    Madre Occidental
12. Border Canyons of
    the Big Bend
13. Mesa Verde National Park
14. Aravaipa Canyon

A climber peers into the depths of the Grand Canyon from the edge of the 7,646-foot-high Shiva Temple on the North Rim.

1

CANYON COUNTRY

THE WORLD BENEATH
THE HORIZON LINE

Roamed, hunted, and tilled by ancient canyon dwellers such as the *anasaázi* (frequently translated to fit the romantic notion of "old ones," but actually a Navajo word meaning "enemy ancestors"), the canyons of North America remained a refuge for Native Americans long after the Anasazi abandoned their canyon realm circa A.D. 1150. What were sanctuaries for indigenous peoples, however, frequently proved to be insurmountable barriers for Spanish explorers, anglo pioneers and settlers, and havens for mountain men, prospectors, surveyors, river runners, geologists, artists, and adventurers. The reason was both simple and complex: Nowhere else in North America was the landscape so daunting as it was in the Great Southwest. And nowhere in the world was the convergence of canyons as magnificent, colorful, and diverse as it was in what would become Arizona, Utah, Colorado, New Mexico, Texas, and, south of the U.S.-Mexico border, Coahuila, Chihuahua, Sonora, Sinaloa, Durango, and Baja California Norte.

Formed during the collision of continental plates called the Laramide Revolution sixty-five to seventy million years ago, the Rocky Mountains and the rivers of white water that were spawned were largely responsible for creating some of the deepest,

1

narrowest, and most storied canyons in the hemisphere. Principal among the cutting agents was the Colorado River and its labyrinth of frothing tributaries. Called the *río colorado* ("red river") for Spanish explorer Juan de Oñate's description of the Little Colorado River in 1604, the Colorado River begins as a patch of snow on the west slope of the Continental Divide at 10,175-foot La Poudre Pass in the Rocky Mountains of Colorado; en route to tidewater at the Gulf of California 1,400 miles downstream, the Colorado River plummets 10,000 vertical feet and, together with the Green River, drains an estimated 244,000 square miles. In the process, the Colorado River helped carve the deep slickrock chasms of Westwater, Canyonlands, and Cataract Canyon in Utah; what, before it was inundated by Lake Powell in 1964, was 186-mile-long Glen Canyon on the Arizona-Utah border; and what is arguably the most awesome single canyon on earth, the Grand Canyon of the Colorado River in Arizona.

The Green River arm of the upper Colorado River drainage system—which some insist is the river's true main stem—begins as glacial runoff from 12,240-foot-high Knapsack Col in Wyoming's Wind River Range. Before it reaches the confluence of the Colorado River in Canyonlands National Park 730 miles downstream, the Green River drops 8,000 vertical feet, and it helped sculpt the gauntlet of canyons formed by Flaming Gorge, Red Canyon, Lodore, Whirlpool, Split Mountain, Labyrinth, and Stillwater. Visited by the mysterious trapper D. Julien in 1836, and later explored by Major John Wesley Powell in 1869, Utah's wilderness of stone remains an Eden for modern river runners and canyoneers.

THE GRAND CANYON OF THE COLORADO RIVER

From Lees Ferry at River Mile 0 on the Colorado River to Pierce Ferry at Mile 277, the Grand Canyon is the single largest canyon in North America; it is also one of the Seven Natural Wonders of the World and the one abyss against which all others are measured. Comprising 2,000 square miles of the most studied and probed geologic strata on earth, it is 277 miles long, 4 to 18 miles wide, and, at its most precipitous point, 6,720 feet deep. Of the seventy-seven

The Grand Canyon of the Colorado
W. J. MINTON; J. W. POWELL

principal tributary creeks and canyons that drain into the Grand
Canyon from its North and South Rims, four stand out as the
longest, deepest, and most astonishing.

Most widely known to foot travelers, perhaps, is the 35-mile-
long, 3,233-foot-deep,[1] mesmerizing labyrinth of Buckskin Gulch/
Paria Canyon. Formed in the kaleidoscopic breaks of Utah's Bryce
Canyon, the Paria River drains nearly 1,000 square miles of the
Paria and Kaiparowits Plateaus and flows into the Colorado River
at Lees Ferry 90 miles below. Used as a travel corridor by Pueblo
people between A.D. 850 and 1100, and kayaked in more recent
times by seasoned "hair boater" and white-water boatman Brad
Dimock, the Paria River created a canyon so narrow and precipitous
that its 1,700-foot-deep Narrows has proved to be a death trap for
hikers foolish enough to enter it during the summer monsoons.

Sixty-one miles downstream from the confluence of the Paria
and Colorado Rivers at River Mile 61, the Little Colorado River enters
the eastern Grand Canyon. Unlike the Paria River, which is one of
many Colorado River tributaries that drain the vast, 6,000-foot-high
Colorado Plateau, the Little Colorado River was born from the

sacred heights of 11,403-foot Mount Baldy in eastern Arizona's White Mountains, what traditional Apache call *dzil ligai* ("white mountains"). The Little Colorado is nearly 200 miles long, and the lower 57 miles form a gorge revered by the Hopi as *sipapuni* ("the opening through which mankind emerged"), which is 3,421 feet deep.[2] Once used by Third Mesa Hopi to reach their sacred salt mines in the Grand Canyon via Salt Trail Canyon, the Little Colorado River Gorge was kayaked by Brad Dimock and Tim Cooper in 1976 and remains an imposing abyss that few other canyoneers make the effort to explore.

Eighty-two miles downstream from the mouth of the Little Colorado River Gorge at River Mile 143.5, Kanab Creek empties its silt-laden waters into the Colorado River. Why it was called a creek instead of a canyon is not known; formed in the 9,000-foot-high ramparts of Utah's Paunsaugunt Plateau, Kanab Creek cuts a 60-mile-long, 3,904-foot-deep[3] corridor of stone that prospectors first used during the gold rush of 1871–72 to reach the Colorado River in the western Grand Canyon. Used by Major John Wesley Powell as the take-out for his second Colorado River Expedition in 1872, Kanab Creek canyon, like the Little Colorado River Gorge, is one of the great, seldom-explored chasms of the American West.

Thirteen miles downstream from Kanab Creek at River Mile 156.5, Havasu Creek empties its aquamarine waters into the same river that early explorers said was "too thick to drink and too thin to plow." Formed by Cataract and Havasu Canyons, Havasu Creek emanates from the forested flanks of 9,256-foot Bill Williams Mountain 75 air miles southeast and at its most profound point is 4,065 feet deep.[4] Still home to a small band of indigenous canyon dwellers known as the *havasupai* ("people of the blue-green water"), this riverine oasis is a must stop for the estimated twenty thousand river runners who raft the Colorado each year—and a dangerous place to tie up a raft during summer monsoons.

Apart from these deep, yawning tributary gorges of the Grand Canyon, many of its seventy-three other confluent creeks and canyons were used as ingress and egress points by the Anasazi during their seasonal migrations between the forested rims and the inner Canyon desert a vertical mile below. Later, during the 1870s,

Kanab Canyon in the Redwall Limestone
THOMAS MORAN; CLARENCE E. DUTTON

View of Marble Canyon
H. H. NICHOLS; J. W. POWELL

prospectors such as Louis D. Boucher, Captain John Hance, and others forged eighty-four different trails along the ancient routes of the Anasazi that have been all but lost to the fifty thousand hikers who march down and struggle up the National Park Service's non-maintained and maintained trails each year. Dedicated Flagstaff, Arizona–based canyoneers, however, have taken a cue from inner Canyon prophet Harvey Butchart, and they devote their energies to tracing out the incipient paths of the Anasazi.

The Colorado River corridor is an altogether different world. Descended by a timeless procession of mythical river runners using hollowed-out canoes, log rafts, wooden boats, and army-surplus river bags—and later traversed on foot in fifty-five days by Bob Marley and Robert Cree in 1980—the Colorado River surges through a passageway of subcanyons within the Grand Canyon that rival the border canyons of Texas's Big Bend in depth and grandeur: 60-mile-long Marble Canyon extends from Lees Ferry at River Mile 0 to the Little Colorado River confluence at Mile 60; 41-mile-long Upper Granite Gorge extends from below Hance Rapids at Mile 77 to Elve's Chasm at Mile 118; 3-mile-long Conquistador Aisle extends from Blacktail Canyon at Mile 120 to Forster Canyon at Mile 123; 4-mile-long Middle Granite Gorge extends from 127 Mile Creek to Bedrock Canyon at Mile 131; the 1-mile-long, 76-foot-wide portal of Granite Narrows, the shortest and narrowest gorge on the lower Colorado River, extends from Helicopter Eddy at Mile 135 to Deer Creek at Mile 136; and 50-mile-long Lower Granite Gorge extends from Three Springs Canyon at Mile 216 to Dry Canyon at Mile 264. Viewed from the North Rim by geologist Clarence E. Dutton in 1882, these corridor canyons remain symbolic mileposts for modern river runners testing the Colorado River's legendary big drops.

COLORADO RIVER TRIBUTARY CANYONS

Principal among the Colorado River tributaries that drain the 130,000-square-mile, four-corner region of the 6,000-foot-high Colorado Plateau are canyons, labyrinths, and narrows cut by the Virgin, San Juan, Dolores, Escalante, Dirty Devil, and Gunnison

Rivers. One of the least explored by canyoneers, perhaps, is the Black Canyon of the Gunnison River. Formed in the 14,000-foot glacial cwms of Colorado's Sawatch Range and Elk Mountains, the Gunnison River took an estimated two million years to cut through the Precambrian schist and granite of Mesa Inclinado to create the Black Canyon of the Gunnison and reach the Colorado River 180 miles below. Draining a 4,000-square-mile area, this brooding chasm is 12 miles long, nearly 3,000 feet deep,[5] plunges 95 feet per mile, and at its narrowest point is only 44 feet wide. The ancestral land of the Ute, the Black Canyon was finally descended in 1882 when Byron H. Bryant and a crew of surveyors from the Denver and Río Grande Railroad took two months to probe the icy chasm with rods and chains.

On the western brink of the Colorado Plateau, Utah's Virgin River trickles down from the alpine heights of the 8,500-foot Kolob Plateau and drains into the Colorado River at the 1,200-foot level of Lake Mead 160 miles below; if visitation figures are any indication, its most engaging stretch is the half-mile-deep, 16-mile-long Virgin River Narrows of Zion National Park. Tributaries of the Virgin River cut canyons no less spectacular, such as 1,700-foot-deep Parunuweap Canyon, 2,000-foot-deep Orderville Canyon, and what have proved to be treacherous, the flash-flood-swept, 1,600-foot-deep Finger Canyons of the Kolob. Revered by the Parrusit band of Southern Paiute, their forbidding canyons were not explored by outsiders until Major John Wesley Powell and his men descended Parunuweap Canyon and probed Virgin River Narrows in 1870; the latter is a canyon pilgrimage that columns of day hikers continue to descend each summer day.

RÍO GRANDE AND RÍO BRAVO DEL NORTE

Draining the east slope of the Continental Divide, the Río Grande forms the Rocky Mountains' second principal cutting agent. Formed beneath an unnamed 12,640-foot pass in Colorado's San Juan Mountains, the Río Grande rumbles through New Mexico's Upper and Lower Taos Box Canyons and meanders south-southeast across the state and the breadth of Texas before reaching the Gulf of

Parunuweap Canyon
BOGERT;
J. W. POWELL

Mexico 1,896 miles from its source; if it weren't for the lower Río Grande's main tributary of the Río Concho draining the east slope of Mexico's Sierra Madre Occidental, the Río Grande wouldn't have the runoff to continue flowing through the canyons of Big Bend National Park. Known south of the U.S.-Mexico border as the Río Bravo del Norte ("Brave River of the North"), it helped create the Texas frontier's most famous canyons: 8-mile-long, 1,100-foot-deep Colorado Canyon;[6] 19-mile-long, 1,500-foot-deep Santa Elena Canyon;[7] 6-mile-long, 2,000-foot-deep Mariscal Canyon;[8] 17-mile long, 2,300-foot-deep Boquillas Canyon;[9] and the 83-mile stretch of water that glides through the 1,600-foot-deep Lower Canyons of the Big Bend.[10]

The ancestral land of the little-known Conchos and Chisos peoples, and later the domain of the Comanche and Lipan Apache, the Big Bend was crossed by a succession of Spanish explorers between 1693 and 1787 and mapped by boundary surveyors during the 1850s. It wasn't until 1881, however, that Texas Ranger Captain Charles L. Nevill and four other Rangers made the first

Falls of Río Bravo
PHIL HOFFMAN LAUDERBACK; WILLIAM H. EMORY

Outward Bound instructor Cilia McClung lines and portages a canoe through the boulder-choked confines of Santa Elena Canyon during a week-long paddle trip through the border canyons of Big Bend National Park.

documented float through Santa Elena Canyon in wooden boats. As the border between Texas and the neighboring Mexican states of Coahuila and Chihuahua, the frontier of the Río Grande–Río Bravo del Norte remains historic river-running country and the haunt of ruthless smugglers.

CANYONS OF THE MOGOLLON RIM

A soaring escarpment of fractured stone nearly 200 miles long, Arizona's 6,000-foot-high Mogollon (pronounced *mogoy-yown*) Rim forms the southern brink of the Colorado Plateau and the natural boundary between two physiographic provinces: the subalpine heights of the Plateau Province to the north, and the Sonoran Desert lowlands of the Basin and Range Province to the south. Incised and drained by a diverse array of creeks and canyons, a few of the canyons of the Mogollon include, among many, Upper Salt River Canyon, the misty plume of Cibecue Falls, the granite narrows of Salome Creek, the plunge pool–choked depths of West Clear Creek, and the boulder-strewn creek bed of Sycamore Canyon. The ancestral realm of ancient peoples such as the Sinagua, and later the dominion of the Yavapai and Western Apache, the canyons of the Mogollon were first explored by Spanish Captain Antonio de Espejo in 1582 and later trapped by mountain man James Ohio Pattie in 1826. Although their physical scale does not compare with that of the Plateau Canyons to the north, the canyons of the Mogollon have challenged explorers ever since Francisco Vásquez de Coronado's men first christened the Salt River the Río de las Balsas ("River of Rafts") in 1540. The handful of canyoneers who've successfully probed this uncompromisingly rugged and beautiful canyon country are well versed in trekking, climbing, rappelling, floating plunge pools, and river running.

CANYONS OF BAJA CALIFORNIA NORTE

A daunting, 175-mile-long spine of raw granite, the 10,154-foot Sierra San Pedro Martír, together with the 6,658-foot Sierra de Juárez, forms the backbone of the 800-mile-long Baja Peninsula. Radiating from the twin horns of Picacho del Diablo ("Peak of the Devil"), the Sierra San Pedro Martír's highest point, is a vortex of unforgivingly rugged mountain canyons unmatched in the Great Southwest for their isolation and stark beauty. Among these soaring *cañones* of granite that climb 8,000 vertical feet from Laguna del Diablo ("Devil's Lake") are La Providencia ("Providence"), Diablito ("Little Devil"), and perhaps the most rugged of them all, Cañon del Diablo ("Canyon of the Devil"). The ancestral land of the little-known Juigrepa, Kiliwa, Akwa'ala, and Ñakipa, the canyons of northern Baja were first explored by Padre Wenceslaus Linck, who traversed the Sierra San Pedro Martír in 1766 and was later described by historians as one of "the great western pathfinders." It wasn't until 1911, however, that cartographer Donald McClain made the first recorded ascent of Picacho del Diablo via Cañon del Cajón ("Box Canyon") after a remarkable journey by foot and skiff from Yuma, Arizona. The handful of savvy canyoneers who still explore these canyons have discovered little has changed in the rugged depths of the Sierra San Pedro Martír since Linck's and McClain's epic journeys.

ISLANDS IN THE GULF STREAM

The Midriff Islands in the Gulf of California form a chain of fifty-five islands, islets, and pinnacles teeming with myriad species of flora and fauna. Naturalists have called them Mexico's Galápagos. None have proved more unforgiving or mysterious to strangers than Isla Tiburón ("Shark Island"), a 750-square-mile Sonoran Desert island that floats in the Sea of Cortés, separated from the coast of Sonora and mainland Mexico by the swift-moving Canal de Infiernillo ("Channel of Little Hell"). The ancestral land of the *tiburones*, the Tiburon Island band of Seri, Tiburon Island was first visited by out-siders in 1700 when Juan Bautista de Escalante raided the Seri and murdered untold numbers on their island redoubt. Grand Canyon boatman George Flavell was murdered on Tiburon Island by the Seri in 1894, as were prospectors John Johnson and George Porter, who ventured onto the island two years later. Canyoneers exploring the small, rugged mountain canyons of Tiburon Island by *panga* ("boat") or sea kayak find them at once haunting and sublime: sublime for their rich biodiversity; haunting because they are now devoid of the Seri, who once completed the natural cycle.

BARRANCAS OF THE NORTHERN SIERRA MADRE OCCIDENTAL

Described by geographers as the southern extension of the Rocky Mountains, the 750-mile-long Sierra Madre Occidental (Western Sierra Madre) arcs southward from Arizona across the Mexican states of Sonora, Chihuahua, Sinaloa, Durango, and Nayarit. Cresting up to 10,585 feet along the Continental Divide, the Sierra Madre ("Mother Mountains") are cleaved by *barrancas* ("canyons") that rival the Grand Canyon of the Colorado River. Popularly known as the Barranca del Cobre ("Copper Canyon"), it is actually a region of distinct canyons cut by the tempestuous rivers of the Sierra

Madre—much the way the Colorado River and its tributaries have cut their own distinct canyons.

Sometimes referred to as Mexico's Grand Canyon, the Barranca del Cobre region's five deepest barrancas link the diminishing old-growth forests of the Continental Divide with the subtropical thorn forests of their western foothills; they are Barranca de Urique, Barranca de Sinforosa, Barranca de Batopilas, Barranca del Cobre, and Barranca de Guaynopa. The ancestral land of the Tarahumara, the northern Sierra Madre Occidental and the region of Las Barrancas del Cobre are sometimes referred to in print as the Sierra Tarahumara. The region was explored by Norwegian Carl Lumholtz, who spent five years between 1890 and 1898 traversing the length of the Sierra Madre to study the indigenous Tarahumara, Tepehuán, Cora, Huichol, and Tarasco. Canyoneers savvy enough to avoid the drug lords who've slashed and burned a stronghold into the "Golden Triangle" region of the Sierra Madre will witness the only place in the Great Southwest—outside of Havasupai, Canyon de Chelly, and several other holdouts—where indigenous canyon dwellers still eke out a largely traditional life in their natural domain.

HOW DEEP ARE THOSE
MEXICAN BARRANCAS?

Pick up and read almost any popular magazine or newspaper account of Mexico's Copper Canyon and its "colorful" Tarahumara Indians, and chances are that two points will be underscored: Copper Canyon is one and a half times deeper than the Grand Canyon and three to four times larger.

Let that sink in for a moment.

As early as 1958, Weldon F. Heald set out to dispel this provocative myth in a *Pacific Discovery* article titled "How deep are those Mexican barrancas?" Among other points, Heald concluded that "the Barranca del Cobre has inspired more false, secondhand, and hearsay information in recent times than any other geographical feature in North America."

Look at the bottom line, and it's not difficult to agree with Heald's view. Of the northern Sierra Madre's five deepest canyons, the Barranca de Urique has been called the deepest, at 6,136 feet deep, while the Barranca de Sinforosa has been measured at 6,002 feet deep. Bottoming out close behind is the 5,904-foot-deep Barranca de Batopilas, the 5,770-foot-deep Barranca de Cobre, and the 5,313-foot-deep Barranca de Guaynopa. For the sake of discussion, let's assume that these estimates—compiled from 1:50,000-scale Mexican Defense Department topographical maps—are accurate. Proponents of the Copper Canyon myth have measured its barrancas from their highest point; yet for reasons that remain cloaked in mystery and the sleight of contour lines, they've measured the Grand Canyon from 7,065-foot Hopi Point—one of the lowest points on the South Rim—and thus concluded that the Grand Canyon is a mere 4,674 feet deep.

Apply the same standards to measuring the depth of the Grand Canyon that have been used to measure the barrancas of the northern Sierra Madre, and you will discover, as Heald did, that the Grand Canyon *is* deeper. Measured from 9,089-foot Crystal Ridge on the North Rim to the 2,369-foot level of Granite

Grand Canyon of the Colorado
W. J. Minton; J. W. Powell

Rapids at Mile 95.6 on the Colorado River, the Middle Granite Gorge section of the Grand Canyon is 6,720 feet deep; measured from the head of the South Canyon at 9,200 feet to the 2,775-foot level below Nankoweap Rapid at River Mile 53, the Marble Canyon section of the Grand Canyon is 6,425 feet deep.

In addition to being touted as one and a half times deeper than the Grand Canyon, the Copper Canyon is usually described as being three to four times larger than the Grand

CANYONS OF THE BIG BEND NATIONAL PARK

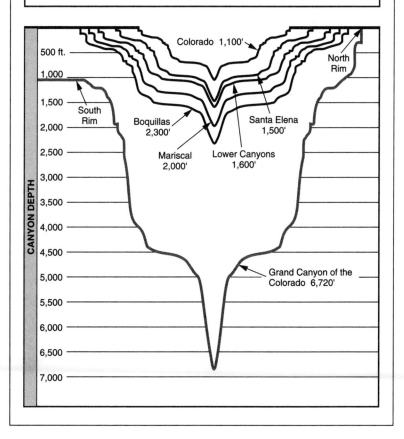

Canyon. Study any of the Mexican topographical maps—or better yet, compare them on foot—and you will see that any of the northern Sierra Madre's stupendous gorges will easily fit lengthwise into the 277-mile-long Grand Canyon; widthwise, their "rims" are not as easily defined as the Grand Canyon's, nor are their walls as sheer or as precipitous. So how do you compare the mountain canyons of the northern Sierra Madre with the plateau canyons of the Colorado Plateau, if, in fact, you can? Using the fluid ancestral boundaries of the Tarahumara, the region of Las Barrancas del Cobre was once estimated to comprise 20,000 square miles, whereas the strict park boundary

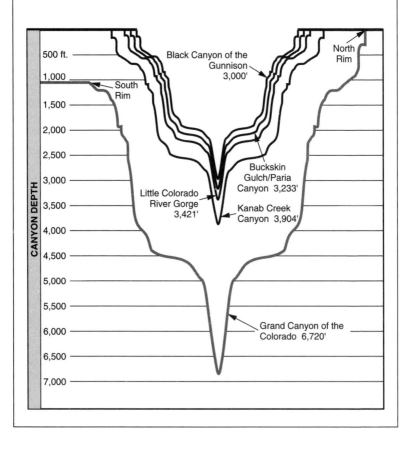

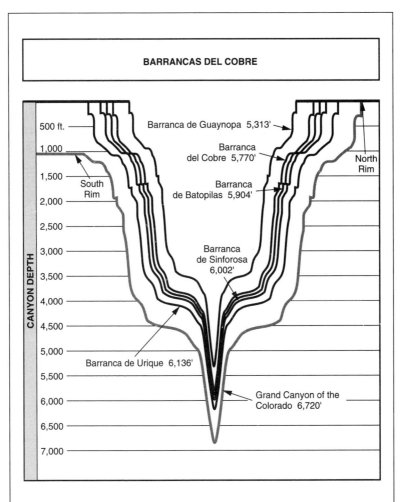

BARRANCAS DEL COBRE

500 ft. — Barranca de Guaynopa 5,313'

1,000 — Barranca del Cobre 5,770'

North Rim

1,500 — South Rim — Barranca de Batopilas 5,904'

2,000 —

2,500 —

3,000 — Barranca de Sinforosa 6,002'

3,500 —

4,000 —

4,500 —

5,000 —

Barranca de Urique 6,136'

5,500 —

6,000 — Grand Canyon of the Colorado 6,720'

6,500 —

7,000 —

CANYON DEPTH

for the Grand Canyon is only 2,000 square miles. However, if you look at the Grand Canyon as just one canyon in a complex labyrinth of gorges that make up the canyons of the Green and Colorado Rivers, as has been done with the barrancas of the western Sierra Madre, then you have to consider how much of the 130,000-square-mile Colorado Plateau region should be entered into the equation. Although no such rule of thumb has been applied to measuring the surface area of the barrancas of the western Sierra Madre, a simple tally of the surface area within the official boundaries of Flaming Gorge National Recreation Area, Rocky Mountain National Park, Dinosaur National Monument, Canyonlands National Park, Glen Canyon National Recreation Area, Black Canyon of the Gunnison National Monument, Zion National Park, Escalante/Grand Staircase National Monument, Buckskin Gulch/Paria Canyon, the Little Colorado River Gorge, Kanab Creek, Cataract/Havasu Canyon, Lake Mead National Recreation Area, and all the other canyons of the Green and Colorado Rivers wedged in between will answer the question of which system of canyons is larger.

Be that as it may, the Río de Piaxtla in the Mexican state of Durango may rival Oregon and Idaho's 7,900-foot-deep Hells Canyon as the deepest canyon in North America; Heald estimated it to be 7,500 feet deep measured from 10,335-foot Cerro Huehueto. But don't rely on large-scale Mexican topographical maps or hearsay. Go explore it for yourself!

FOOTNOTES

[1] Measured from 6,333-foot Lees benchmark on the Paria Plateau to 3,100 feet at the Colorado River confluence at River Mile 0. The Navajo Sandstone is 1,700 feet thick at the Narrows.

[2] Measured from 6,146-foot Cape Solitude to 2,725 feet at the Colorado River confluence at River Mile 61.5.

[3] Measured from 5,779-foot Kanab Point on Kanab Plateau to 1,875 feet at Kanab Rapid at River Mile 143.5.

[4] Measured from 5,840-foot Ukwall Point on Great Thumb Mesa to the Colorado River confluence at River Mile 156.5.

[5] Measured from 8,563-foot Green Mountain to 5,600 feet at the Gunnison River.

[6] Measured from benchmark 3465 to 2,200 feet at river's edge.

[7] Measured from the 3,883-foot summit of Mesa de Anguilla to 2,100 feet at river's edge.

[8] Measured from the 3,932-foot summit of Mariscal Mountain to 1,900 feet at river's edge.

[9] Measured from the 4,134-foot summit of the Sierra del Caballo Muerto ("Dead Horse Mountains") to 1,760 feet at river's edge.

[10] Measured from the 3,100-foot summit of the Bullis Gap Range to 1,460 feet at river's edge.

2

PHYSIOGRAPHY

THE LAY OF THE LAND

The magnificent physical geography of the Great Southwest's canyon country is molded by five of the continental United States' sixteen principal physiographic provinces. First identified by Major

Delicate Arch and the sandstone turrets of Arches National Park, Utah are some of the most spectacular landforms in canyon country.

John Wesley Powell in 1895 and later interpreted by physiographer and geomorphologist Armin Kohl Lobeck in 1932 to encompass North America, they include the Southern Rocky Mountain Province, the Colorado Plateau Province, the Basin and Range Province, the Mexican Highland Province, and the Lower California Section of the Sierra-Cascade-Coast Mountain Province. The

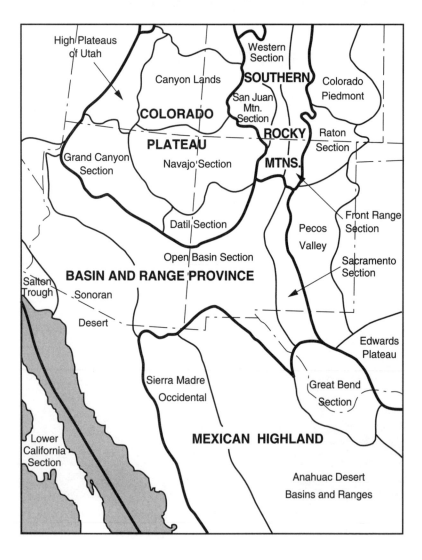

canyons of the Great Southwest are further defined by a diverse cross section of biotic communities found elsewhere throughout the world; these universal biomes, or life zones, include Desert Scrub, Grassland, Chaparral, Woodland, Forest, and, in the loftier reaches of the Southwest's volcanic peak, Tundra. But first let's traverse the lay of the land to see what beckons over the horizon line.

SOUTHERN ROCKY MOUNTAIN PROVINCE: HEADWATERS TO THE SEAS

Rearing above the Colorado Plateau Province to the west and the Great Plains Province to the east, the Southern Rocky Mountain Province is characterized by Colorado's fifty-four snow-capped peaks that soar to 14,000 feet or more above sea level. Stretching from the Wind River Range of Wyoming to the San Juan Mountains of southwestern Colorado, the tundra-covered glacial ramparts of the Continental Divide form the backbone of North America, and from here the headwaters of rivers such as the Colorado, the Green, and the Río Grande cut a labyrinth of canyons en route to divided seas.

COLORADO PLATEAU PROVINCE: THE HEART OF CANYON COUNTRY

Comprising an estimated 130,000 square miles, the 6,000-foot-high Colorado Plateau encompasses the four-corner region of Utah, Arizona, Colorado, and New Mexico and contains some of the most spectacular scenery, terrain, and geology in North America. Incised by the Green River, the Colorado River, and their tumultuous tributaries, the Colorado Plateau is covered by the wind-whipped Great Basin Desert and smaller colorful tracts known as the *Desierto Pintado* ("Painted Desert"), the Coral Pink Sand Dunes, and the Bisti Badlands. Its imposing, multihued escarpments include Vermillion Cliffs, Echo Cliffs, and Book Cliffs, and its cloud-piercing laccolithic peaks take names such as the Henry Mountains, the Abajo Mountains, and Navajo Mountain. Named after the indigenous bands of Southern Paiute who dwelled among them, its sweeping plateaus include Shivwits, Unikaret, Kanab, Kaibab, and Kaiparowits Plateaus. Its most sacred landmarks, revered by traditional Native Americans such as the *Diné* (commonly known as the Navajo), include, among many, Sunset Crater, Shiprock, Monument Valley, Rainbow Bridge, and Canyon de Chelly.

Within such a spectacular natural setting, which includes the cliff dwellings and ball courts of Chaco Canyon, Hovenweep, and Mesa Verde, one might find it difficult to believe that the canyons of the Colorado Plateau Province rival the scale, grandeur, and sublimity of its towering landforms. But this is the heart of canyon country, because here nature has formed the Grand Canyon of the Colorado River—arguably the largest, deepest, and most awesome canyon in North America. And here spring snowmelt and torrential summer monsoons have carved earth's narrowest canyons, among them the slot canyons of Paria Plateau's Buckskin Gulch, Kaibito Plateau's Antelope Canyon, and Waterpocket Fold's Burro Wash.

BASIN AND RANGE PROVINCE: DESERT CANYON COUNTRY

Characterized by rugged, northwest-trending fault-block mountain ranges and separated by broad, intervening desert basins and valleys, the Basin and Range Province comprises an estimated 300,000 square miles and forms one of North America's largest physiographic provinces. Emanating from southern Oregon, it sweeps across most of Nevada, southeastern California, and western Utah and slashes across southern Arizona and New Mexico before bottoming out in the Big Bend frontier of Texas and Coahuila. Its most infamous landforms, however, are not its supernal mountains such as 13,063-foot Wheeler Peak in the Snake Range of Nevada's Great Basin National Park or even its biological "islands in the sky" such as the Chiricahua, Santa Catalina, and Santa Rita Mountains in southeastern Arizona; nor do they include the lower Colorado River gorge of Black Canyon, the stone canyons of the Superstition Mountains, the barrancas of the Western Sierra Madre foothills, or the border canyons of Big Bend. Rather, they are the merciless deserts that separate these alluring landforms. The haunting expanses and scorching temperatures of Death Valley in California's Mojave Desert, the *Camino del Diablo* ("Road of the Devil") in Arizona's Sonoran Desert, and the *Jornada del Muerto* ("Journey of the Deadman") in New Mexico's Chihuahuan Desert claimed the lives of hundreds of—some historians estimate more than two thousand—spaniards, pioneers, immigrants, and forty-niners who perished of thirst in the white pall of summer heat during the late 1800s.

When Spanish conquistador Francisco Vásquez de Coronado first stared into the frightful, empty maw of what would become the American Southwest in 1540, it was pronounced a *despoblado* ("uninhabited land"). Since that *entrada* in 1540, the vast region of the Basin and Range Province earned a reputation as the Great American Desert, although it comprises five distinct deserts that also define its canyons: the Great Basin, Mojave, Sonoran, Chihuahuan, and Painted Deserts.

Swallowing over half a million square miles, the deserts of North America left their mark on four of the Great Southwest's five physiographic provinces—none more so than the Basin and Range Province—and many of their canyons, as well as in nine states west of the 100th meridian and seven states south of the U.S.-Mexico border. It is a daunting sweep of mysterious lands, indigenous people, legends too tough—or too peculiar—to die, and Sun Belt boomtowns fueled by a lust for dwindling water more precious than oil or gold.

Highest among the deserts that burn across the Great Southwest—and torch its canyons in mid-June—is the 158,000-square-mile Great Basin Desert. The ancestral lands of the Ute and Southern Paiute, this mile-high desert covers the northern half of the Basin and Range Province and much of the Colorado Plateau Province. Smallest among its deserts is southeastern California's 54,000-square-mile Mojave Desert, with an average elevation of 2,000 to 4,000 feet. It's home to one of the deadliest rattlesnakes in North America and formed the ancestral realm of legendary runners such as the Mojave and Chemehuevi, who could traverse a hundred miles of burning salt pan between two sunrises. Lowest and hottest among its deserts is the 106,000-square-mile Sonoran Desert, a daunting refuge for ancient peoples such as the Hia Ced

O'odham ("People of the Sand," commonly known as the Sand Pápago), who quenched their parched lips with sand roots and cactus fruit. Ranging in elevation from sea level to 4,500 feet, the Sonoran Desert covers southwestern Arizona and much of the Mexican state of Sonora and extends across the 800-mile-long Baja Peninsula (including Baja California Norte and Baja California Sur). Largest among its deserts is the 175,000-square-mile Chihuahuan Desert, with an average elevation of 3,000 to 6,000 feet. It links the Basin and Range Province with the Anahuac Desert Basin and Range Section of the Mexican Highland Province it traverses.

MEXICAN HIGHLAND PROVINCE: BARRANCA COUNTRY

Described by geographers as a southern extension of the Rocky Mountains, the Sierra Madre Occidental (Western Sierra Madre) arcs southward from Arizona across the Mexican states of Sonora, Sinaloa, Chihuahua, Durango, and Nayarít in one continuous 750-mile-long push. Bordered on the west by the gulf coast of the Sea of Cortés, the Sonoran Desert, and the Sinaloan Thorn Forest, the Western Sierra Madre looms to over 10,000 feet along the Continental Divide. Cleaved on its steep western front by mile-deep barrancas, the Sierra Madre are drained by rivers named for native peoples, such as the Río Mayo and Río Yaqui, and other such as the Río Batopilas and Río Urique, which carved their namesake barrancas. Because of its nearly impenetrable barrancas and its isolation, the Western Sierra Madre remained virtually lost to the outside world until the completion of the Chihuahua al Pacífico railroad in 1921. Until its extirpation during the 1960s, the Mexican grizzly bear was still hunted in the western Sierra Madre, as was the Mexican gray wolf, which roamed as far south as Durango until the late 1970s; today, the Sierra Madre Occidental still provides a dwindling natural refuge for the jaguar. Home to the largest, most traditional groups of indigenous peoples remaining in North America, including the Tarahumara, Cora, and Huichol, the Western Sierra Madre contains perhaps the most seldom-visited canyons in North America. The east slope of the Sierra Madre Occidental forms the headwaters of the Río Conchos. En route to recharging the Río Grande/Río Bravo del Norte, the verdant, rolling foothills and plains of the upper Río Conchos give way to the Anahuac Desert of the Mexican Highland Province. This Central Basin, as it is also known, bridges the gulf between the Western Sierra Madre and the commanding presence of the *Sierra Madre* Oriental (Eastern Sierra Madre).

COAST MOUNTAIN PROVINCE: THE FORGOTTEN PENINSULA

Linked to California's Sierra Nevada Range by northern Baja's Sierra de Juárez and Sierra San Pedro Mártir, the Lower California Section of the Coast Mountain Province is a physiographic extension of California's 10,800-foot San Jacinto Mountains. Cresting to 10,154 feet, the Sierra San Pedro Mártir, together with the 6,658-foot Sierra de Juárez, forms an impressive 175-mile-long double range that plummets to sea level on its eastern front, creating stone barrancas that are virtually cut off from the modern world and all but the hardiest of canyoneers and rock climbers. In what was once home to indigenous peoples such as the Akwa'ala, Nakipa, and Juigrepa, now only furtive bands of *borrego cimarón* ("wild sheep," or desert bighorn) and dense groves of palm trees (*Washingtonia filifera*) seem to thrive in Baja California Norte's rugged barrancas.

3

BIOGEOGRAPHY

MERRIAM'S LIFE ZONES
AND PLANT DISTRIBUTION

No study of canyon country would be complete without an overview of the geographic distribution of plant life that forms North America's biotic communities.[11] Determined by many factors such as elevation, temperature, latitude, climate, slope exposure, and soil composition, these life zones change as one moves from lower to higher elevations and from southern to northern latitudes. Today, these universal biomes are defined as Desert Scrub, Grassland, Chaparral, Woodland, Forest, and Tundra; in North America; they are also known as the Lower Sonoran, Upper Sonoran, Transition, Canadian, Hudsonian, Subalpine, and Alpine Tundra life zones.

Among the early gun-toting naturalists who studied and profiled these biotic communities, Clinton Hart Merriam is perhaps best known today. Born in New York in 1855, the thirty-three-year-old Yale graduate and doctor of medicine foresook a promising medical career to pursue biogeography. Financed on a shoestring by the Department of Agriculture in 1889, Merriam had little more than $600 to travel from Washington, D.C., to northern Arizona and equip two months of rugged fieldwork with horses, burros, tents, food, supplies, and a camp cook. Setting out from Flagstaff, Arizona, on July 29, after a sixteen-day rail journey from the nation's

Located in the Sonoran Desert life zone, a senita cactus and palo blanco tree form one of the unique plant communities in the canyons of Tiburón Island, Sonora.

capital, Merriam's small party established a base camp at Little Spring near the 8,250-foot level on the north side of the San Francisco Mountains. According to Merriam, the highest mountain in the Arizona territory was selected "because of its southern position, isolation, great altitude, and proximity to an arid desert." From their camp, which lay tucked in a grove of quaking aspen and ponderosa pine, Merriam's party made forays up the mountain to collect plants, birds, and mammals and observed the succession of life zones change as they climbed through what Merriam called the Neutral or Pine Zone, (Central) Canadian or Balsam Fir Zone, (Central) Hudsonian or Spruce Zone, and Subalpine or Timberline Zone to the tundra of the Alpine Zone, which covered the rocky 12,633-foot summit of Humphrey's Peak. Here, Merriam and his assistant, Vernon Bailey, observed eight or nine bighorn sheep, one of the last bands to roam the San Francisco Mountains before they were hunted out. From their Little Spring base camp, Merriam's party also made two journeys across the Painted Desert, descending

San Francisco Peaks
RANDOLPH; J. W. POWELL

through what Merriam called the Piñon Zone to the Desert area of the Little Colorado River, and another journey to the bottom of the Grand Canyon. It was their first reconnaissance of the Painted Desert, however, that almost proved the expedition's undoing.

For naturalists who studied such matters, Merriam's party was seemingly unprepared for the blistering August heat as they rode north on horseback from Grand Falls across the burning lava and shimmering sweep of Painted Desert searching for water holes that appeared on their maps but turned up dry in the mirage of red sand and rocky mesas. In *The Last of the Naturalists: The Career of C. Hart Merriam*, author Keir B. Sterling wrote: "For three days they went without water, and nearly died of thirst. Elizabeth [Merriam's wife] had taken with her a small tube of cold cream, which she carried around her neck, and which she used to moisten her lips. After several days, the men borrowed some lest their lips become blackened and dry." Fate smiled on the ill-fated party when, nearly deranged from thirst, they met a Hopi elder 16 miles north of the ancient Hopi settlement of Oraibi; he led them to a mud hole so vile that their horses wouldn't drink from it. Using an old rubber hose, the Hopi man siphoned water out of the mud hole and put it in a pot. Merriam brewed coffee with the muddy water to mask its foul taste, a common practice among explorers such as Major John Wesley Powell, who had his own share of close calls while exploring the parched reaches of the Colorado Plateau. Refurbished by the "strange tasting" coffee and providential helping of goat's milk given to them by the Hopi elder, they pushed on to Oraibi, where they gorged on sweet melons, blue corn, and water provided by the Hopi there.

Hailing from the cool, moist climes of New York's Adirondack Mountains, Merriam and his party had been pushed to the limits of desert thirst in the Painted Desert, commenting later that "the heat was intense and much suffering was occasioned by want of water." (Extreme temperatures and dehydration continue to afflict ill-prepared canyoneers throughout the Great Southwest's canyon country to this day.) In spite of the hardships Merriam's party endured, including a trip into the Grand Canyon that Merriam made on a lame knee carrying "some traps + a bag of pancakes + our guns," they covered over 500 miles on horseback and foot in twenty-four days of traveling, reportedly discovered twenty new species and subspecies of mammals, and redefined the concept of life zones in North America.

As his model for studying geographic plant distribution, Merriam profiled the 7,983-foot vertical relief between the summit of the San Francisco Mountains and the Little Colorado River at Grand Falls near the 4,650-foot level; within this abrupt stretch of 25 linear miles, Merriam identified the principal biotic communities found throughout North America, including the canyon country of the Great Southwest.

Had Merriam had the time, funding, and inclination to conduct a similar biogeographic survey from the North Rim of the Grand Canyon to the Colorado River, he would have noted that all but the Timberline and Alpine Zones existed between the rim and the river. Because the Grand Canyon has five of the seven principal life zones found in North America, it's a good multitiered cross section to use as a guide for identifying its biotic communities as well as those found elsewhere throughout canyon country: from Canyonlands National Park in the north to the Barranca del Cobre region of the Sierra Madre Occidental in the south, and from the border canyons of Big Bend in the east to the canyons of the Sierra San Pedro Mártirs in the west.

For example, if you were to hike down the North Kaibab Trail from the North Rim to Phantom Ranch—or, for that matter, from summit to base of one of southeastern Arizona's biological "islands in the sky," such as 9,157-foot-high Santa Catalina Mountains—you would pass through five of Merriam's seven life zones. In terms of biogeography, Merriam was the first to compare such a journey to the equivalent of traveling from the Canadian to the Mexican border: "In descending from the [Coconino] plateau to the bottom of the [Grand] cañon," Merriam wrote, "a succession of temperature zones is encountered equivalent to those stretching from the coniferous forests of northern Canada to the cactus plains of Mexico."

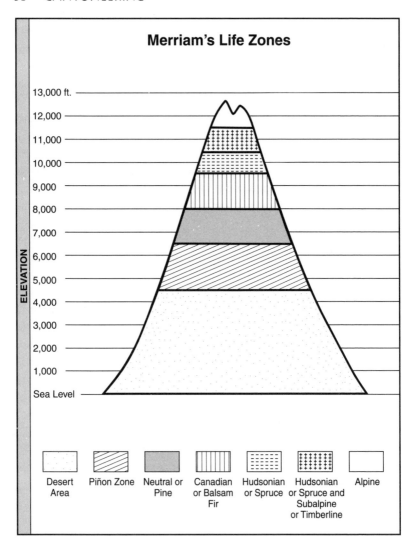

MERRIAM'S LIFE ZONES

Merriam's Zone	Modern Name[12]	Elevation[13]

Alpine   Alpine Zone   11,500 to 12,633 feet

(Timberline to the summit of San Francisco Mountains and loftier peaks found elsewhere throughout the Great Southwest.)

Indicator life-forms:[14] alpine tundra, San Francisco Peaks groundsel, wood betony, lichen, sedge, woodrush, alpine fescue, tundra bluegrass, liverwort.

Subalpine or   Same   10,500 to 11,500 feet
Timberline

Indicator life-forms: bristlecone pine, stunted Engelmann spruce, dwarf juniper, gooseberry currant.

Hudsonian or Spruce   Hudsonian   9,500 to 11,500 feet

(The highest point on the North Rim is 9,240 feet at the head of South Canyon.)

Indicator life-forms: Engelmann spruce, alpine fir, blue spruce, quaking aspen, limber pine, maple.

Canadian or   Canadian   8,000 to 9,500 feet
Balsam Fir

Indicator life-forms: Douglas fir, white fir, white pine, limber pine, water birch, quaking aspen.

Neutral or Pine   Transition   6,500 to 8,000 feet

Indicator life-forms: ponderosa pine, Chihuahuan pine, apache pine, alligator juniper, gambel oak, alder.

Piñon Zone   Upper Sonoran   4,500 to 6,500 feet

Indicator life-forms: piñon, juniper, emory oak, Mexican blue oak, alligator juniper, manzanita, mountain mahogany, chaparral, wait-a-minute bush, grama grass, and Great Basin Desertscrub.

MERRIAM'S LIFE ZONES

Merriam's Zone	Modern Name[12]	Elevation[13]

Piñon Zone (cont.)

Great Basin Desert. Indicator life-forms: piñon, juniper, galleta grass, big sagebrush, black sagebrush, plains prickly pear cactus, Mormon tea, Indian rice grass, tumbleweed, black brush.

The Desert Area	**Lower Sonoran**	**Sea level to 4,500 feet**

(The lowest point in the Grand Canyon that Merriam's party reached was approximately 2,500 feet at the Colorado River.)

Within the Desert Area, or Lower Sonoran life zone, there are four sub-divisions of particular interest to canyoneers exploring the far reaches of canyon country: Riparian Woodland, Lower Sonoran Desert, Mojave Desert, and Chihuahuan Desert.

Riparian Woodland (extends to Canadian life zone). Indicator life-forms: cottonwood tree, coyote willow, mesquite, catclaw, redbud, hackberry, tamarisk, box elder, poison ivy, maidenhair fern, red brome grass, ocotillo, barrel cactus, Utah century plant, narrowleaf yucca, bear grass.

Lower Sonoran Desert. Indicator life-forms: saguaro cactus, barrel cactus, cholla cactus, prickly pear cactus, organ pipe cactus, senita cactus, cardón cactus, ironwood tree, palo verde tree, velvet mesquite tree, elephant tree, boojum tree, ocotillo, desert agave, maguey, jojoba, creosote bush, brittle bush.

Mojave Desert. Indicator life-forms: Joshua tree, smoke tree, honey mesquite, screwbean mesquite, Mojave yucca, blue yucca, ocotillo, diamond cholla cactus, teddy bear cholla, creosote bush, Parry saltbush, Mojave sage, woolly bursage, white bursage, burro bush, white shadscale, catclaw, arrow weed, big galleta.

Chihuahuan Desert. Indicator life-forms: ocotillo, creosote bush, tarbush, soaptree yucca, banana yucca, honey mesquite, prickly pear cactus, sotol, buffalo gourd, Apache plume, peyote, lechuguilla, candelilla, desert marigold.

LIFE ZONE CANYON GUIDE

Unlike the Grand Canyon, many other canyons lie within one or two distinct life zones. Southern Arizona's Aravaipa Canyon, for instance, lies within the Lower Sonoran Zone, though it supports a distinct Riparian Woodland community because it has one of the only free-flowing streams in the Sonoran Desert. Utah's Buckskin Gulch, in contrast, lies completely within the Great Basin Desert. Black Canyon of the Lower Colorado River lies within the Mojave Desert, and the canyons of Big Bend lie within the Chihuahuan Desert. Still other canyons such as the Barranca del Cobre region of the Sierra Madre Occidental, and Cañon del Diablo in Baja's Sierra San Pedro Mártir, mirror the diversity and complexity of life zones found in the Grand Canyon. In journeying from Satevó in the lower reaches of the Barranca de Batopilas to the Continental Divide region of the Sierra Madre Occidental, you would approximate the

Canyon—105 miles above the mouth of the Pecos
PHIL HOFFMAN LAUDERBACK; W. H. EMORY

biogeographical trek from the bottom of the Grand Canyon to the North Rim, though you would be traveling through the distinct Mexican subdivisions of North America's life zones: Lower Colorado Subdivision of the Sonoran Desert Scrub Zone, Sinaloan Deciduous Forest of the Forest Zone, Madarean Evergreen Woodland of the Woodland Zone, and Petran Montane Conifer Forest of the Forest Zone. Conversely, if you were to climb from the sere playa of Devil's Lake through Cañon del Diablo to the summit of Picacho del Diablo of the Sierra San Pedro Mártir, you would make a journey through a succession of life zones comparable to both the Barranca del Cobre and Grand Canyon treks; in Baja California Norte, those zones have been identified as the Lower Colorado River Subdivision of the Sonoran Desert Scrub Zone, the California Chaparral of the Desert Scrub Zone, and the Sierran Montane Conifor Forest and Sierran Subalpine Conifer Forest of the Forest Zone.

FOOTNOTES

[11] The biological diversity of canyon country would not be complete without the colorful abundance of birds, mammals, reptiles, fish, and insects that complete each life zone; however, it is beyond the scope of this book to treat the subject in depth.

[12] Within these principal life zones, there are many distinct subdivisions that change markedly as you journey north, south, east, and west of the Grand Canyon. See Brown, *Biotic Communities;* Lowe, *Arizona's Natural Environment;* MacMahon, *Deserts;* Merriam, "Results of Biological Survey"; and Whitney, *Western Forests* in the Bibliography.

[13] Elevations are approximate, as they change with latitude and slope exposure.

[14] Not all life-forms listed exist in the Grand Canyon, though they appear elsewhere throughout canyon country.

4

GEOLOGY

READING THE ROCKS

What C. Hart Merriam's formative work did for conceptualizing the life zones of North America, Clarence Edward Dutton's geological surveys were said to have done for understanding the stratigraphy of the Grand Canyon and the Colorado Plateau regions. A cigar-smoking Yale graduate and Civil War ordnance expert, Dutton was assigned to survey the Colorado Plateau region between 1875 and 1881. From his exhaustive field investigations, first for the Powell Survey and later for the U.S. Geological Survey, Dutton penned four enlightening monographs: *Report on the Geology of the High Plateaus of Utah, The Physical Geology of the Grand Canyon District, The Tertiary History of the Grand Canyon District,* and *Mount Taylor and the Zuñi Plateau.* Illustrated with superlative line drawings by Thomas Moran and William Henry Holmes, *The Tertiary History of the Grand Canyon District* was recognized as Dutton's magnum opus; he described the canyon's stupendous geology not only in glowing scientific terms but with a literary voice that introduced the Grand Canyon to the world:

> The common notion of a cañon is that of a deep, narrow gash in
> the earth, with nearly vertical walls, like a great and neatly cut

trench. There are hundreds of chasms in the [Colorado] Plateau Country which answer very well this notion. Many of them are sunk to frightful depths and are fifty to a hundred miles in length. Some are exceedingly narrow, as the cañons of the forks of the Virgin, where the overhanging walls shut out the sky. Some are intricately sculptured, and illuminated with brilliant colors; others are picturesque by reason of their bold and striking sculpture. A few of them are most solemn and impressive by reason of their profundity and the majesty of their walls, but . . .

The north summit horn of 10,154-foot Picacho del Diablo in Baja California Norte offers canyoneer Jason Lohman a craggy bivouac perch after an arduous multiday trek and ascent.

The Grand Cañon of the Colorado is a great innovation in modern ideas of scenery, and in our conceptions of grandeur, beauty, and power of nature. As with all great innovations it is not to be comprehended in a day or a week, nor even a month. It must be dwelt upon and studied, and the study must comprise the slow acquisition of the meaning and spirit of that marvelous scenery which characterizes the Plateau Country, and of which the great chasm is the superlative manifestation.

The Grand Canyon, looking east from Toroweap
J. W. POWELL

Based on such eloquence, one would assume that Dutton was high-minded, serious, and reverant. A letter written to Major John Wesley Powell during Dutton's Colorado Plateau expedition, however, underscored Dutton's sense of humor. He wrote, "How high and steep and rough a hill a mule could roll down without getting killed."

The Grand Canyon of the Colorado River is still recognized as the "superlative manifestation" of canyon country; as such, it's the best guide for identifying its geological divisions and subdivisions, as well as those of canyons found elsewhere throughout the Great Southwest. Seen from its North and South Rim vistas, the Grand Canyon's geological time line is an open book to all those who care to trace the course of a falling drop of water from rim to river. Nowhere else in canyon country is the stratigraphy as colorful, grandiose, and easily identifiable for discerning rim-bound tourists and ardent canyoneers as it is at the Grand Canyon. In hiking down the 14-mile-long North Kaibab Trail, you descend through twelve principal geological formations that date from 250 million to 2,000 million years ago. They are the Kaibab Limestone, Toroweap Formation, Coconino Sandstone, Hermit Shale, Supai Group, Redwall Limestone, Muav Limestone, Temple Butte Limestone, Bright Angel Shale, Tapeats Sandstone, Grand Canyon Supergroup, and Vishnu Group.

Grand Canyon boatmen have developed several mnemonics to memorize nine of the Grand Canyon's principal geological formations. One goes like this: "Kissing Takes Concentration; However, Some Require More Breath And Tongue." In descending order from rim to river, the formations are Kaibab, Toroweap, Coconino, Hermit, Supai, Redwall, Muav, Bright Angel, Tapeats.

GRAND CANYON OF THE COLORADO RIVER

A Stairstep Canyon. Although the Grand Canyon's tributaries include gorges such as the Little Colorado River, chasms such as Kanab Creek, slot canyons such as Buckskin Gulch, and narrows such as Deer Creek, it has been called "the world's best example of a stairstep type of canyon" for the graduated terraces that separate its sheer walls.

Pinnacles in Kaibab formation
W. H. HOLMES; C. E. DUTTON

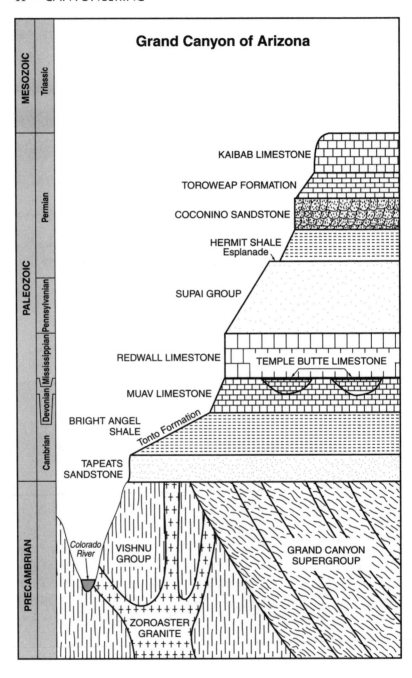

Grand Canyon of Arizona

Though the Grand Canyon may be easily recognized as a stair-step canyon by many of the five million tourists who visit it each year, its origin is far more controversial. Scientific debates on the topic have raged for the last century, but it is generally agreed that two momentous actions, and many geological events, formed the Grand Canyon: a great upheaval of the earth's surface 1.7 billion years ago; and, with the advance and retreat of perhaps seven oceans, the corrasion, or downward cutting, of the Colorado River and its tributaries for a period of six to thirty million years.

GRAND CANYON ROCK FORMATIONS

Name	Age

Kaibab Limestone   250 million years

Description: Named for the Kaibab band of Southern Paiute who inhabited the North Rim's Kaibab Plateau, this Permian layer of gray and ivory-colored marine limestone is embedded with chert and bears the marks of ancient sea life such as sponges, coral, and brachiopods. Three hundred to 500 feet thick, the Kaibab Limestone caps the Kaibab Plateau and forms the Grand Canyon's North and South Rims—and the sheer escarpments that greet visitors peering over the brink.

First Encountered: Mile 0, North Kaibab Trail.

Toroweap Formation   255 million years

Description: Named after *toro-weap*, the Kaibab Paiute word for "gully" or "wash," this Permian layer of gray limestone and yellow sandstone bears the impressions of marine fossils. The Toroweap Formation is 250 to 450 feet thick and erodes back from the sheer wall of the Coconino Sandstone.

First Encountered: Mile .5, North Kaibab Trail.

Coconino Sandstone   260 million years

Description: Named for the ancient Coconino people who inhabited the South Rim's Coconino Plateau, this Permian layer of bone-colored sandstone is made of fossilized sand dunes that bear tracks of scorpions, insects, reptiles, and amphibians. Three hundred to 350 feet thick, the Coconino Sandstone crowns the Coconino Plateau and forms one of the most precipitous bands of cliffs in the Grand Canyon. Spectacular freestanding rock spires called temples—many named by Dutton after Eastern deities such as Mencius, Confucius, and Buddha—are largely composed of Coconino Sandstone; this layer has been nicknamed the "coke" by climbers who scale its temples.

First Encountered: Mile 1, Coconino Overlook, North Kaibab Trail.

Hermit Shale   265 million years

Description: Named after French-Canadian miner and hermit Louis D. Boucher, this Permian layer of red siltstone and shale is comprised of freshwater deposits bearing traces of reptile tracks and thirty-five different fossilized plants. At 250 to 1,000 feet thick, the Hermit Shale sometimes forms an abrupt, 100-foot-thick, overhanging barrier for climbers trying to scale Coconino Sandstone temples such as Isis and Zoroaster.

First Encountered: Mile 1.2, North Kaibab Trail.

Supai Group   285 million years

Description: Named for indigenous canyon dwellers called the *havasupai* ("people of the blue-green water"), this multitiered layer of Permian and Pennsylvanian red shale and limestone is composed of floodplain deposits that bear the tracks of reptiles and mammals. Six hundred to 1,350 feet thick, the Supai group is made up of four different formations: Esplanade, Wescogame, Manakacha, and Watahomigi.

First Encountered: Mile 1.5, above Supai Tunnel, North Kaibab Trail.

Redwall Limestone   335 million years

Description: Called the "blue lime" by Grand Canyon prospectors during the 1800s, this Mississippian layer of gray limestone is stained red by runoff from the Supai and bears the patterns of marine invertebrates such as coral and brachiopods. Five hundred to 750 feet thick, the Redwall Limestone forms a daunting cliff and an intimidating, nearly impenetrable barrier to inner canyon foot travel. Veteran canyoneers, when inquiring about a route description, often ask, "How do you get through the Redwall?" (This question is also frequently asked about the Kaibab Formation and Coconino Sandstone.)

First Encountered: Mile 2.5, Redwall Bridge, North Kaibab Trail.

Niches, or panels, in the Redwall Limestone
W. HOLMES; C. E. DUTTON

Temple Butte Limestone   350 million years

Description: Named for 5,308-foot Temple Butte in the eastern Grand
Canyon, this Devonian layer of purple limestone and sandstone bears
the impressions of coral, brachiopods, and armored fish. One hundred
to 450 feet thick, the Temple Butte Limestone forms a slope and
dolomite cliff that erodes back from the Muav Limestone.

First Encountered: Not easily encountered on the North Kaibab Trail.

Muav Limestone   535 million years

Description: Named for a Southern Paiute word, perhaps that of an
elder named Muavigaipi ("Mosquito Man"), this Cambrian layer of
gray limestone shows traces of brachiopods and trilobites. Four hundred to 1,000 feet thick, the Muav Limestone forms the headwaters of
spectacular Grand Canyon cataracts such as Tapeats, Thunder River,
and Deer Creek Falls.

First Encountered: Mile 3.8, below Eye of the Needle, North Kaibab Trail.

Bright Angel Shale   530 million years

Description: Taken from the name Major John Wesley Powell bestowed
on Bright Angel Creek, this Cambrian layer of green limestone, siltstone, and sandstone bears the imprints of crustaceans. Three hundred
to 450 feet thick, the Bright Angel Shale forms the broad terrace of the
Tonto Plateau. Of all the Grand Canyon's geological layers, the Tonto
Plateau is the most heavily used by canyoneers for east-west inner
canyon foot travel.

First Encountered: Mile 4.7, above Roaring Springs, North Kaibab Trail.

Tapeats Sandstone   545 million years

Description: Named for Major Powell's Paiute guide named Tumpeats
("Small Rocks"), this Cambrian layer of dark brown sandstone is 150 to
250 feet thick and forms the precipitous outer rim of the Tonto Plateau
and the Inner Gorge. Unlike the sheer, nearly unbreachable walls of
the Kaibab Formation, Coconino Sandstone, and Redwall Formation,
numerous access routes can be found through the Tapeats' band of
horizontal ledges by skilled and observant canyoneers who are not
unnerved by exposed, unroped climbing.

First Encountered: Mile 5, Tapeats Narrows, North Kaibab Trail.

Grand Canyon Supergroup   1,200 million years

Description: Characterized by red sandstone, black lava, and orange
shale, this complex layer of Precambrian rock is also called the "Great
Unconformity," because it does not conform to the layer-cake sequence
of Grand Canyon stratigraphy. Ranging in depth from 120-foot-thick
Sixtymile Formation to 4,200-foot-thick Galeros Formation, the grand
Canyon Supergroup also includes the Kwagunt Formation, Cardeñas
Lava, Dox Formation, Shinumo Quartzite, Hakatai Shale, and
Bass Formation.

First Encountered: Mile 6, above Cottonwood Camp, North Kaibab Trail.
Also seen when viewing 5,401-foot Cheops Pyramid from the South
Rim's Maricopa Point.

Vishnu Group   2,000 million years

Description: Name derived from the Sanskrit name Vaisnava, one of
the supreme triad of Hindu gods that also includes Brahma and Siva

(or Shiva), this glistening wall of black gneiss and quartzite is 800 to 1,200 feet thick and forms the Inner Gorge.

First Encountered: Mile 10, The Box, North Kaibab Trail.

BUCKSKIN GULCH AND PARIA CANYON

Inclosed Meanders, Narrows, and Slot Canyons. In 1915, geologist Herbert E. Gregory began a survey by pack mule of the vast, unmapped region of the Kaiparowits Plateau in southern Utah. Known only to the indigenous Navajo and Southern Paiute and a handful of tough cattlemen and prospectors trying to scratch out a living in the desolate slickrock country, its striking landforms and canyons include, among many, Waterpocket Fold, Circle Cliffs, Escalante River, Last Chance Creek, Wahweap Creek, Glen Canyon, and the Paria River. Bypassed by the Powell and Wheeler Surveys, Gregory surveyed a 5,400-square-mile area that was all but lost to the outside world in order to "determine routes, to locate waterholes, and to select areas where geologic study could be undertaken." One such study that Gregory undertook in this remote tract of the United States was of the twisting, narrow defiles he called inclosed meanders. Eighty-two years later, this area would become known as Escalante–Grand Staircase National Monument.

In *The Kaiparowits Region: A Geographic and Geological Reconnaissance of Parts of Utah and Arizona,* Gregory wrote: "All the canyons are sinuous to a degree very much greater than indicated on topographic maps. Close-set meanders with horseshoe curves and goosenecks are common, and the traverse of many of a canyon involves passing to right and left about towering buttresses with turns approaching 180°." Many canyons in the Colorado Plateau region have the characteristics of inclosed meanders, among them Antelope Canyon, Parunuweap Canyon in Zion National Park, and the Upper and Lower Black Box of San Rafael Swell. But today they are more popularly known as narrows or slot canyons. Apart from the wind- and water-sculptured symmetry that characterizes many slot canyons, narrows, and inclosed meanders, they have a near miraculous luminescent beauty that comes from refracted sunlight playing off their concave, overhanging walls. But there is also a dark side to these canyons, which resemble fissures cleaved in the earth's crust more than deep, wide plateau canyons such as the lower half of Paria Canyon, the Little Colorado River Gorge, Kanab Creek, and the San Juan River. These serpentine corridors of raw stone can form instantaneous death traps for unwary canyoneers during summer monsoons.

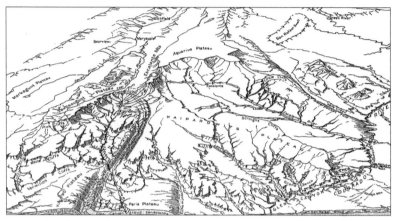

Generalized view of the Kaiparowits Region, looking north from the Utah-Arizona boundary line
HERBERT E. GREGORY AND RAYMOND C. MOORE

Two basic actions worked in concert to produce the narrows, slot canyons, and inclosed meanders of the Colorado Plateau: a tremendous upheaval of the Colorado Plateau approximately ten million years ago; and the tenacious corrasion through the region's strata of soft sandstone by steep, sediment-bearing, flood-swollen creeks following their ancestral watercourses.

The 42-mile-long journey through the Buckskin Gulch–Paria Canyon Primitive Area on the Utah-Arizona border takes you through the narrows of Buckskin Gulch and the plateau canyon of the Paria River. While slithering, wading, scrambling, and trekking from Wire Pass to Lees Ferry, you descend through seven stratigraphic formations that span an estimated 120 million to 200 million years: Carmel Formation, Page Sandstone, Navajo Sandstone, Kayenta Formation, Moenave Formation, Chinle Formation, and

Moenkopi Formation. Most important to canyoneers, perhaps, is the 1,700-foot-thick Navajo Sandstone; it's through this immense layer of ancient sand dunes that Buckskin Gulch has carved a magnificent 10-mile-long inclosed meander that forms a virtually escapeproof corridor during tempestuous flash floods. The Narrows of Zion National Park have also been worn through this same Lower Jurassic layer of Navajo Sandstone.

CANYONLANDS AND ARCHES NATIONAL PARKS

Plateau Canyons, Needles, Mazes, and Arches. The geologic story of the plateau canyons of Canyonlands National Park is also one of upheaval, erosion, and deposition. Stand on any of the promontories of 6,240-foot Island in the Sky, and you can see the web of canyons cut by the corrasive forces of the Green and Colorado Rivers; they produced the deep, winding plateau canyons of Labyrinth, Stillwater, and Cataract. Stand on the lip of 5,680-foot Dead Horse Point at dawn, and in the amber light you can trace

Standing up country
J. W. POWELL

out the layers of stone that the Colorado River cut through as it sought a path to the sea. From rim to river, they are Kayenta Sandstone, Wingate Sandstone, Chinle Formation, Moenkopi Formation, Cutler Formation, and Honaker Trail Formation. Put in at Potash and row the meanders of the Colorado River toward the maelstrom of spring runoff surging through the Big Drops of Cataract Canyon, and you will view these same compressed layers of stone in a very different light.

But Canyonlands' geology is not limited to its plateau canyons; it is as well known for its magnificent landforms that soar above the horizon line—what C. Gregory Crampton called "standing up country." Eroded in Permian layers of cross-bedded Cedar Mesa Sandstone and Organ Rock Shale, The Maze is said to be one of the most seldom visited areas in the United States, but there are many such regions in the West; the Arizona Strip section of the western Grand Canyon, the canyons of northern Baja's Sierra San Pedro Mártir, the vast dunes of frontier Sonora's *El Gran Desierto,* and southwestern Arizona's San Cristóbal Valley come immediately to mind. Yet none have the characteristics of The Maze, a 30-square-mile labyrinth of twisting narrows, cul-de-sacs, hoodoos, fins, and soaring walls of stone bearing the ancient murals of the Anasazi. And no one described such country better than Edward Abbey when he wrote:" the least inhabited, least inhibited, least developed, least improved, least civilized . . . most arid, most hostile, most lonesome, most grim, bleak, barren, desolate, and savage quarter of the state of Utah—the best part by far."

The Needles country also fits this bill, where wind, rain, and frozen water have carved banded spires, grabens, and arches in the Cedar Mesa Sandstone. But nowhere else on earth has nature formed the proliferation of natural arches found in Arches National Monument. Here, in the heart of slickrock country, the cataclysmic forces of the earth's movement combined with wind, rain, and extreme air and ground temperatures—vacillating from below freezing to 160° Fahrenheit—to fracture, dislocate, and sculpt fifteen hundred stone rainbows in Jurassic layers of Entrada Sandstone during the last 100 million years.

SOME OF THE OTHERS

Barrancas. The deep barrancas of the Sierra Madre Occidental do not conform to the layer-cake stratigraphy of the Plateau Canyons. Trek through the Barranca del Cobre region between the desert lowlands of Satevó and the forested Continental Divide region of Creel and you will travel through Cenozoic layers of igneous rock ranging from intrusive granite to extrusive andesite and riolite.

Mountain Canyons. The same holds true for the stone canyons of the Sierra San Pedro Mártir. Climb from the sere desert *bajadas* at the mouth of Cañon del Diablo to the craggy windblown summit horns of 10,154-foot Picacho del Diablo and you will scramble over hard crystallized rock that looks and feels like granite but is Cenozoic-aged intrusive grandorite and tonalite.

Rim Canyons. Scramble, stumble, trek, wade, and swim down the canyons of the Mogollon Rim such as Sycamore Canyon—which George Wharton James described as a "miniature Grand Canyon" in 1917—the West Fork of Oak Creek, Wet Beaver Creek, and West Clear Creek and you will be descending through some of the same rock formations found in the upper levels of the Grand Canyon. As you move east along the Mogollon Rim, however, the geologic composition of rim canyons varies widely to that of the Mescal Limestone, Dripping Spring Quartzite, and Ruin Granite of the Upper Salt River Canyon.

5

CANYONEERS

NATIVE AMERICANS, SPANIARDS, AND ANGLOS

NATIVE AMERICANS

The ancient people who dwelled among the canyons of the Great Southwest were diverse, hardy, and remarkable; they adapted to extreme environments that ranged from the blistering canyons of the Big Bend region to the snow-lashed escarpments of the Colorado Plateau and the Western Sierra Madre. Among the many venerable cultures that once thrived there were the Anasazi, Hakataya, Mogollon, Fremont, Shoshonean, and Chichimeca, and each left indelible traces of their passage. Mural-sized pictographs of men and deer painted with natural dyes—some believe by the hands of giants—adorn the roofs of caves in the remote canyons of central Baja's Sierra de San Francisco. Petroglyphs of shamans, kachinas, and coyotes are found etched in stone throughout the canyons and mesas of the Colorado Plateau. And giant earth carvings, variously known as intaglios and geoglyphs, of rattlesnakes, mazes, and vision circles still emerge from the stark *bajadas* and creosote flats of the Colorado River Desert. Captivating yet mystifying, these and notched calendar sticks are the only known recordings that ancient Native Americans left behind before many—such as the Anasazi,

Inhabited by the Anasazi until the 1400s, Square Tower House in Mesa Verde National Park, Colorado, is one of the most magnificent cliff dwellings in canyon country.

who ranged throughout the Grand Canyon and four-corners region of the Colorado Plateau—mysteriously abandoned their canyon domain circa A.D. 1150.

Were it not for the ancient cliff dwellings still clinging to canyon walls throughout the Great Southwest, from the Barranca de Sirupa in the Sierra Madre Occidental to Mesa Verde National Park, we would not know that indigenous people actually dwelled in a canyon realm and did not merely wander through in search of adventure as modern man now must. To the dismay of traditional Native Americans—and this author—archaeologists have plundered many such dwellings, including sacred caves, graves, kivas, and pueblos, collecting and cataloging pirated booty and bones for the "scientific record."

If one turns to the descendants of the ancient canyon dwellers to trace out their canyon journeys, however, there is a wealth of knowledge to be gleaned from them, as well as from early ethnographers who worked side by side with Native American "informants" to

Native American canyon dwellers
J. W. POWELL

document their traditional lifeways before they were lost or defiled by the onslaught of European immigrants. Coming from a rich oral tradition, Native Americans passed on vibrant creation stories and legends from one generation to the next in sacred chants and ceremonies—many that lasted four days and nights or more. Lacking a fluency in Native American linguistics or an intimate knowledge of their day-to-day culture, modern canyoneers can still study early ethnographic accounts to gain a broader understanding and knowledge of indigenous canyon life and travel.

Compiled from their own tellings and from the books, journals, and accounts of explorers, ethnographers, and adventurers, the following is a sketch of the original canyoneers.

BY FOOT

Foremost among the ancient canyoneers in what would become the American Southwest were the Anasazi. They blazed many declivitous rim-to-river routes throughout the Grand Canyon region, and they used them during seasonal migrations between hunting grounds on the forested North and South Rims and small agricultural plots they tilled along the Colorado River. Traveling over some of the most daunting terrain on earth, the Anasazi climbed and descended 5,000 vertical feet or more wearing flimsy yucca fiber sandals to protect their feet from skin-ripping Muav limestone.

Once compared with the Grand Canyon Anasazi for their traditional lifeways, the Tarahumara of the Barranca del Cobre region of the Sierra Madre Occidental were no less prodigious canyon travelers than the Anasazi. Known among themselves as the *rarámuri* ("foot runners"), they have long been considered the greatest long-distance runners in the world for their multiday kickball races, which were reported to cover as much as 200 miles of rugged canyons and mesas in forty-eight hours. As early as 1902, Carl S. Lumholtz wrote that "a Tarahumare will easily run 170 miles without stopping." The Tarahumara have been credited with many seemingly incredible running feats. And American runners who scoffed at such notions had their doubts laid to rest when a fifty-five-year-old Tarahumara grandfather named Victoriano Churro, sponsored by American canyoneer Richard Fisher, won the 1993

The Tarahumara are the last of the true canyon dwellers, living in the Barranca del Cobre region of Mexico's Sierra Madre Occidental. Numbering between forty thousand and sixty thousand, they are the largest and most traditional indigenous group remaining in North America.

Leadville 100-mile endurance race in twenty-two hours and two minutes wearing a pair of handmade *huaraches* (sandals).

BY HORSEBACK AND FOOT

One of the most extraordinary, yet tragic, eras of Native American canyon travel took place in the 1880s during what the U.S. government called the "Apache Wars." Forcefully dislocated from their ancestral land in southeastern Arizona and northern Mexico, the Chiricahua Apache were moved to a reservation at San Carlos, Arizona. Unable to resist the lure of their homelands and freedom, Geronimo and a small band of Chiricahua escaped and made repeated raids into the heart of the northern Sierra Madre 250 miles south to rustle Mexican cattle and horses. But time was running out for the Chiricahua, and before Geronimo made his final surrender at Skeleton Canyon, Arizona, on September 4, 1886, he and a desperate, hungry, and courageous band of thirty-seven Chiricahua led five thousand American troops on a cunning chase through the barrancas and *quebradas* ("broken country") of the Río Bavispe, Sierra del Tigre, and Río Aros region of the northern Sierra Madre. Decades after Geronimo and the Chiricahua were incarcerated at

Comanche signal of discovery
H. H. NICHOLS; J. W. POWELL

Fort Pickens, Florida, rumors persisted on both sides of the U.S.-Mexico border that a group of "lost Apache" were living out their final days in a redoubt of canyons in the Sierra Madre.

The Comanche were also respected and feared for their equestrian prowess. Driven south by government troops protecting settlers traveling west across the continent to fulfill their Manifest Destiny, the Comanche made strikes against American and Mexican settlements on both sides of the Río Grande–Río Bravo del Norte in the Big Bend frontier of Texas, Coahuila, and Chihuahua. Fording the river on horseback between the soaring walls of Mariscal and Santa Elena Canyons, the Comanche conducted raids as far south as the Mexican state of Zacatecas during what non-Indians came to fear as September's Comanche Moon.

BY SCRAMBLING AND CLIMBING
Modern man is not alone in his quest to stand on the lofty summits of pinnacles and mountains throughout the Great Southwest. Used by the Anasazi for roasting mescal hearts, the remains of stone *yanta* ovens dating between A.D. 900 and 1100 can still be seen on the summit of the Grand Canyon's 7,646-foot Shiva Temple. Ruins and other artifacts, such as flint scrapers for cleaning the hides of deer and bighorn sheep, have also been seen atop 7,721-foot Wotan's Throne, 7,431-foot Guinevere Castle, 7,281-foot Elaine Castle, and two dozen other freestanding buttes, mesas, and temples. It's irrefutable evidence that the Anasazi were making difficult and dangerous ascents in the Grand Canyon 500 to 600 years before Spaniards first tried to descend to the bottom of it.

BY WOODEN FOOTBRIDGE
The best-known Anasazi footbridge in canyon country can be seen in the Grand Canyon by observant river runners at River Mile 43 on the Colorado River. Reportedly discovered by surveyor Gordon Denipah while flying with helicopter pilot Lynn Roberts, the fragile truss spans a dangerous gap high above the Colorado River. Studying its unique position in the river corridor between Eminence Break and Point Hansbrough led boatman Kenton Grua to think that it might connect a route up from the Colorado River to the rim

Signals to a traveler on a ridge say, "Who are you?"
H. H. Nichols; J. W. Powell

of the Redwall Limestone. After several attempts at exposed climbing on crumbly rock, Grua and boatwoman Ellen Tibbetts reportedly climbed out to 4,484-foot Point Hansbrough. If, indeed, the Anasazi used the intimidating route, they were well accustomed to harrowing ascents where one misstep meant a deadly plunge.

BY HANDMADE ROPE

The discovery of ancient talismen in a ceremonial cave below the South Rim in 1954 suggests that the Anasazi were fearless climbers who may have also used ropes to reach precarious perches, summits, and caves. Using pitons and ropes to rappel off the rim into the cave, speleologists and archaeologists were surprised to discover split-twig figurines made by the ancient canyoneers, perhaps as effigies for a successful hunt. One party member wrote that they needed "considerable mountaineering skill and equipment" to enter the cave.

Without the benefit of tenuous footbridges, wooden ladders, and toeholds carved in stone (popularly known as Moki steps), it's conceivable that the Anasazi used handmade ropes, perhaps braided from yucca fiber, to reach such shrines. The Hopi were known to use ropes to reach their sacred salt deposits in the Grand Canyon at the turn of the century and still use ropes to gather eaglets from the walls of distant canyons. Traveling on sacred pilgrimages from Third Mesa 90 miles east, Hopi men from the Sun, Sand, and Coyote Clans descended the Little Colorado River Gorge via Salt Trail Canyon to reach the eastern Grand Canyon. Without the benefit of modern ropes or rappel harnesses, the fearless Hopi descended hand-over-hand by rope over an inner rim of the canyon to collect salt; once reverent offerings were made, they made the dangerous climb back up their dangling ropes with cumbersome loads of sacred salt.

BY SWIMMING, RAFT, AND CANOE

If we relied on Hollywood conceptions of Native Americans, we would not know that they knew how to swim. Even desert-dwelling people such as the Mojave were skilled swimmers, as well as formidable long-distance runners. They forded the lower Colorado

River to reach nearby villages and to travel throughout the far reaches of the land to trade with canyon-dwelling people such as the Hualapai.

The Chisos people of the Big Bend region forded the border canyons of the Río Grande by wading and swimming. They also developed a unique method for hunting waterfowl. Wearing gourd masks, swimmers floated up to wary ducks and caught them by grabbing their webbed feet from beneath the surface of the water.

One of the earliest, best-known accounts of a Native American running the Colorado River through the Grand Canyon was told by Wi-ki, a Hopi Antelope chief, to ethnographer J. Walter Fewkes before 1894. Using a hollowed-out canoe made from a cottonwood trunk, Ti-yo's legendary river journey took him through the Grand Canyon to the underworld and the dawn of Hopi migration.

Ethnographic accounts of the Havasupai and Hualapai describe their proficiency in crossing the treacherous currents of the Colorado River in the western reaches of the Grand Canyon. Either by swimming or by paddling a log raft carrying their meager supplies in front of them, the Havasupai and Hualapai crossed the river to trade—and war—with the Uinkaret and Shivwits bands of Southern Paiute living on the north side of the Colorado River. Such river

The Needles (Mojave Range)
J. J. YOUNG; LT. JOSEPH C. IVES

crossings were often made during late summer, when the Colorado River was relatively warm and its level low.

Dwelling on San Estéban Island, Tiburón Island, and the Gulf Coast of Sonora, the Seri navigated the dangerous currents of the Sea of Cortés on reed *balsas* made from carrizo grown at isolated locations throughout their Sonoran Desert homelands. One stand of carrizo grew in a remote canyon of Tiburón Island, and during the 1960s, Thor Heyerdahl journeyed there to research the Seri's use of reed balsas for his *Ra Expedition.*

SPANIARDS

Not long after Spanish conquistador Hernán Cortés landed in the Mexican port of Veracruz in 1519, he crushed the Aztec empire, and thereafter, missionaries and conquistadors began pushing the northern frontier of New Spain. In quest of souls and gold, they traversed many of the most rugged canyons in the Great Southwest under the auspices of the Spanish crown: from the Sierra Madre Occidental to the canyons of the Big Bend, and from the Sierra San Pedro Mártir to the canyons of the Mogollon Rim. However, where Native Americans had learned to live in, climb in, travel through, and navigate the canyons of the Colorado Plateau region, the Spaniards encountered their most uncompromising obstacles.

The first Spaniard credited with "discovering" the Grand Canyon was García López de Cardeñas, and he was also the first non-Indian to recognize it as a barrier. Led to the South Rim by Hopi guides in September 1540, Cardeñas sent Juan Galeras, Pablo de Melgosa, and a third man into the depths of the Grand Canyon to search for a route to the Colorado River, which they called the Río Tizón ("Firebrand River"). But after three days of fruitless struggle, the weary men emerged from the canyon defeated, prompting Cardeñas to write what was still to be echoed by exhausted canyoneers more than four centuries later: "What appeared to be easy from above was not so, but instead very hard and difficult."

During their failed expedition to pioneer a new route from Santa Fe, New Mexico, to Monterey, California, in 1776, Fathers Francisco Domínguez and Silvestre Escalante also came to an

During the sixteenth century, Spanish soldiers and conquistadors traversed many of the rugged canyons of New Spain—what later became known as northwest Mexico and the American Southwest.

impasse in canyon country. Returning to Santa Fe after an arduous five-month-long journey across the Colorado Plateau, Domínguez and Escalante were trapped at the base of Echo Cliffs because they were unable to ford the Colorado River on a log raft. Finally, on November 2, one of the padres' men found a route through the imposing wall of Echo Cliffs, prompting them to write their own canyon missive that is cried out by flash-flood victims to this day: ¡Salsipuedes! ("Get out if you can!").

Where Cardeñas and Domínguez and Escalante failed to meet the challenges of canyon country, Padre Francisco Tomás Garcés succeeded. Having crossed the grim expanses of both the *Camino del Diablo* ("Road of the Devil") and the Mojave Desert to reach Mission San Gabriel in California, Garcés was a seasoned explorer. The Franciscan padre became the first non-Indian to descend into the Grand Canyon at Havasupai on June 20, 1776; in his journal, Garcés wrote: "I went five leagues east, two northeast, and three north, the last four of these over very bad (*malisima*) ground through some cajones [canyons] the most profound. . . . On one side is a very lofty cliff, and on the other a horrible abyss (*voladéro*). . . . I arrived at a rancheria which is on the Río Jabesúa [Havasu Creek]." Garcés completed his extraordinary journey by returning to Mission San Xavier del Bac in Tucson, rivaling the difficult explorations made by padre Francisco Eusebio Kino across the Sonoran Desert. Tragically, the renowned explorer was beaten to death later that same year by Yuma Indians after he made the first recorded midsummer traverse of the Camino del Diablo.

In the heart of the Chihuahuan Desert far to the southeast, Pedro de Rábago y Terán's horseback expedition set out to traverse the daunting canyons of the Big Bend two decades before Garcés's murder. Dispatched by viceroy Pedro de Rivera to scout locations for presidios that would protect the settlements of New Spain from depredations by the Comanche and Apache, Rábago's expedition included sixty-five soldiers and ten Indians and was the first known party to cross the heart of what the Spaniards feared as the merciless *despoblado* ("uninhabited land").

Led by what he callously called "a pagan Indian . . . guide," padre Wenceslaus Linck's party was the first known expedition to

Canyon country traversed by Domínguez and Escalante
H. H. NICHOLS; J. W. POWELL

traverse the hard-rock spine of Baja's Sierra San Pedro Mártir in 1766, following a route through tortuous canyons that cleaved the imposing east face of the sierra. Linck wrote on March 17: "We traversed most of the way on foot, since to ride horseback would have exposed us to the danger of rolling over cliffs."

ANGLOS

The surfeit of adventures and exploits by Anglo canyoneers has filled scores of classic volumes from Major John Wesley Powell's *Explorations of the Colorado River of the West and Its Tributaries: Explored in 1869, 1870, 1871, and 1872* to Paul Horgan's two-volume edition of *Great River: Río Grande in North American History;* from C. Gregory Crampton's *Standing Up Country: The Canyonlands of Utah and Arizona* to Carl S. Lumholtz's *Unknown Mexico: A Record of Five Years' Exploration Among the Tribes of the Western Sierra Madre, in the Tierra Caliente of Tepic and Jalisco, and Among the Tarascos of Michoacán.* Unfortunately, it is beyond the scope of this book to provide more than a thumbnail sketch of these colorful eras.

BY FOOT
During the late 1800s, miners and raconteurs such as Captain John Hance, Louis D. Boucher, William Wallace Bass, Seth B. Tanner, and others constructed eighty-four different trails along the faint paths of the Anasazi in order to reach their diggings, glory holes, cabins, stills, and orchards in the depths of the Grand Canyon. Today, popular rim-to-river trails such as the Tanner, Hance, Boucher, and Bass still bear the names of these early canyoneers.

Next to John Wesley Powell, the most famous early explorers of the Grand Canyon were Ellsworth and Emery Kolb. They came to the Grand Canyon in 1902 and spent a lifetime photographing it and exploring it by foot, rope, and wooden boat. Among many historic forays, including photographic expeditions by foot and pack burro to Cataract Canyon and the Little Colorado River Gorge, the Kolb brothers are credited with discovering the seasonal cataract of Cheyava Falls in 1908, making the first motion picture of a Colorado River expedition in 1911–12 (from Green River, Wyoming, to

Canyoneer Louise Teal crosses a plunge pool in Buckfarm Canyon, Arizona.

Needles, California), and searching for the missing river-running honeymooners Glen and Bessie Hyde in 1928. In 1937, Emery made the first and second recorded ascents of 7,646-foot Shiva Temple two weeks before the American Museum of Natural History expedition proclaimed that it made the first ascent on September 16.

Many canyoneers came and went, but none left their footprints throughout the Grand Canyon the way Northern Arizona University math professor J. Harvey Butchart did. He made his first hike down the South Kaibab Trail in 1945, and in the five decades that ensued before his retirement from canyoneering at age ninety, Butchart discovered 116 rim-to-river routes, pieced together 164 breaks through the Redwall Limestone, and climbed 83 buttes and temples.

For legions of zealous canyoneers who took Butchart's cue, he became the prophet of inner canyon foot travel, and he inspired many. Among them was Welshman Colin Fletcher; in 1962, Fletcher made the first recorded trek from one end of the Grand Canyon to the other. Whereas Fletcher's trek made use of Butchart's route descriptions, aerial food drops, the Tonto Trail, and other trails on

Upper Cataract Creek
J. J. YOUNG; LT. J. C. IVES

the south side of the Colorado River, Ginny Taylor's and Chris Wuerhman's self-contained party was the first known to traverse the virtually trailless, seldom-explored terrain below the Grand Canyon's North Rim. Commencing their five-week journey in November 1976 with a descent of the Nankoweap Trail, Taylor and Wuerhman spent twenty-nine days methodically piecing together a traverse below the North Rim all the way to Dutton Point on 7,661-foot Powell Plateau. From journey's end at nearby Muav Saddle, the weary canyoneers had to hoof it all the way back to the North Kaibab Trail and descend to the river before returning to civilization at the South Rim via the Hermit Trail on day thirty-four.

As difficult as Taylor's and Wuerhman's North Rim adventure was, and as inspirational as Fletcher's South Rim journey proved to be for book buyers, neither party had really gone from one end of the Grand Canyon to the other. Enter dory boatman Kenton Grua, known among canyon cognoscenti as "the Factor." Following a route along the south side of the Colorado River, Grua trekked the estimated 600 canyon miles from Lees Ferry at River Mile 0 near the head of Marble Canyon to Grand Wash Cliffs near Pierce Ferry at Mile 277 in an elapsed time of thirty-six days during March and April 1976. As enviable as Grua's journey was for canyoneers limited to weekend forays of "Butcharting," it wasn't until 1980 that much of the Colorado River corridor was traversed on foot; that honor went to Bob Marley and Robert Cree of Phoenix, who trekked upstream from Diamond Creek 225 river miles to Lees Ferry in fifty-five days during the early fall of 1980.

It would be easy to limit this overview to the Grand Canyon region, but to do so would slight veteran canyoneers who have penetrated the far corners of canyon country. Among them is Kentucky-born Richard Fisher, whose canyon travels have taken him around the world to Bolivia, Greece, China, and Tibet. Closer to home, Fisher has made difficult descents by foot and raft of the Barranca del Cobre region of the Sierra Madre Occidental and technical descents by rope and raft of Arizona's Mogollon Rim canyons. But Fisher has gone most modern canyoneers one better. Fisher developed a running program for the Tarahumara that enabled them to demonstrate their legendary running prowess at American ultra-distance mountain races such as the Leadville 100, Wasatch 100, Los Angeles Crest 100, and Western States 100. And that is no easy undertaking. Just to get the Tarahumara to the starting line requires a rugged journey by truck to and from a third-world wilderness and is akin to taking traditional Native Americans out of the last century and depositing them in a crowd of modern athletes dressed in running shoes that cost the equivalent of a month's wages in the Western Sierra Madre.

Poke around the narrows and slot canyons of the Colorado Plateau in Utah, and the name Michael Kelsey keeps surfacing. Like Fisher, Kelsey's canyon and mountain journeys have taken him around the world. Thumb through one of the Utah native's canyon guidebooks, and black-and-white self-portraits highlight Kelsey's two decades of canyon explorations throughout the labyrinth of tributary canyons and narrows draining into the Green and Colorado Rivers: from Diamond Creek Narrows in the western Grand Canyon to Black Dragon Canyon in Utah's San Rafael Swell and the Escalante River in Escalante–Grand Staircase National Monument.

Mention the word *Escalante*, and Rudi Lambrectse comes to mind. The Holland-born canyoneer, guidebook author, and photographer has trekked the main stem of the Escalante River and probed its tributary gulches, narrows, hollows, arches, Moki steps, alcoves, dunes, natural bridges, water pockets, cracks in the wall, and waterfalls. In this same mythic slickrock canyon country, twenty-year-old vagabond, poet, and romantic Everett Reuss mysteriously disappeared in 1934.

BY HORSEBACK AND FOOT

No stranger to canyon country, Mormon missionary and explorer Jacob Hamblin made the first recorded journey completely around the Grand Canyon in 1862, crossing the Colorado River at opposite ends of the canyon at what would become known as Lees Ferry and Pierce Ferry. In 1870, Hamblin led Major John Wesley Powell across the forlorn Arizona Strip country to meet with the Shivwits band of Southern Paiute in order to learn the fate of William Dunn and Seneca and Oramel Howland, three disgruntled boatmen who left Powell's 1869 Colorado River expedition at Separation Rapid.

Major Powell and his Paiute guide
W. L. S.; J. W. POWELL

One of the most uncanny cattle drives in the history of the West was probably that made by Mormon polygamist John D. Lee. Reportedly married to seventeen women from across the territory, Lee made the first recorded descent of Paria Canyon in 1871; it was a journey that took Lee and his men eight days, because they were driving sixty head of cattle through the narrows, quicksand, and ice of Paria Canyon to establish the first reliable ford across the Colorado River, at what would become known as Lees Ferry.

About the time that Lee and his seventeenth wife, Emma, were settling in at the mouth of Paria Canyon, at what Emma called Lonely Dell, news broke out that gold had been discovered at the confluence of Kanab Creek and the Colorado River in the western Grand Canyon. Scores of fever-struck miners made the difficult 60-mile trek down the length of Kanab Creek canyon in the hope of hitting the mother lode. Walter Clement Powell, a cousin of Major Powell's and a member of his second Colorado River expedition, wrote a series of letters to the *Chicago Tribune* in 1872 describing the Kanab Creek gold rush:

> Miners report every trail to the Colorado Cañons crowded with men seeking the new Eldorado. The washes leading down, such as Pipe Springs, Kanab, and Grand Wash are the only practical routes to the river. All sorts of outfits arrive. Some come in wagons, some on horseback, muleback, afoot, and one in a donkey cart. . . . They expected the rich leads of that never-to-be-forgotten year of '49. The excitement broke out so suddenly, the fever ran so high, that people crowded to the auriferous shore [of the Colorado River] without food, without knowledge of mining, without proper implements. After prospecting for a time, and getting but a few fine grains of gold, provisions run out, hopes fall, starvation stares them in the face.

Horse meat proved to be a reliable ration during such hard times; traveling independent of one another across the Mojave Desert decades apart, both Jedediah Smith and Kit Carson were reduced to eating horse flesh in order to survive. So one can only imagine how much horse meat was eaten by famished miners in the depths of Kanab Creek canyon. But that was not the reason American surveyors killed their horses near Boquillas Canyon in the Big Bend frontier during 1881. Fearing that their mounts would be stolen by Comanches, surveyors clubbed nine horses to death; Big Bend National Park's Sierra del Caballo Muerto ("Deadhorse Mountains") was named after the incident. Canyonland's Deadhorse Point was named after a similar incident when a band of "broomtails," or mustangs, died of thirst after cowboys left them penned up in a desert corral 2,000 feet above the Colorado River.

Horse thieves working both sides of the Grand Canyon rarely stopped long enough to corral their stolen mounts; a rope pen made from lariats, called a remuda, was far more efficient. According to one National Park memo, horse thieves stole horses in Utah, drove them across the rugged terrain of the eastern Grand Canyon via the Nankoweap, Butte Fault, and Tanner Trails, changed their brands, then sold them in Arizona. It was the same route that 125 cowboys and Indians on horseback tried using in 1924 to drive a herd of mule deer from the North Rim to the South Rim; their preposterous roundup fell apart, however, when the deer scattered wildly before reaching the head of the Nankoweap Trail.

A cartographer for the U.S. Geological Survey, François Emile Matthes, had far more success crossing and recrossing the Grand Canyon on horseback in 1902 in order to produce the USGS's first topographical map. Called the *Bright Angel Quadrangle,* the area was no mean feat to survey. According to J. Donald Hughes's *The Story of Man at the Grand Canyon,* Matthes's party swam the Colorado River above Bass Rapid to retrieve William Wallace Bass's boat; they needed it to guide their horses and mules across the Colorado River in order to reach the North Rim. The journey, the first recorded rim-to-river-to-rim crossing, took six days; en route back to the South Rim, Matthes's party blazed a horse trail down Bright Angel Canyon, crossing Bright Angel Creek ninety-four times before reaching the Colorado River.

Almost a decade before Matthes's party topped out on the South Rim, Norwegian doctor, explorer, and ethnographer Carl Sofus Lumholtz spent five years traversing the length and breadth of the Sierra Madre Occidental on horseback before reaching the Tarascan Indians in the Mexican state of Michoacán. In his two-volume edition *Unknown Mexico,* Lumholtz wrote that he told thirty Tarascan that he wanted to photograph them so other people would know "how you look and how you are." The black-and-white images Lumholtz brought back from his unprecedented traverse of the Western Sierra Madre remain a timeless collection of the indigenous Tarascan, Huichol, Cora, Tepehuán, Tarahumara, and O'ob who dwelled in the sierra's loftiest reaches and deepest barrancas.

BY LOG RAFT

No overview of canyoneers would be complete without the story of James White, because his is the most fantastic and controversial account of running the wild Colorado River through the Grand Canyon. On September 7, 1867, the Colorado miner drifted up to the banks of Callville, Nevada (now submerged beneath Lake

Mead), on a crude log raft made from three cottonwood logs lashed together with rope. On the verge of starvation, the weary, sunburned White claimed to have spent fourteen days navigating the Big Cañon in an audacious bid to escape hostile Ute Indians. In a letter written to his brother Josh on September 26, White said that he kept from starving during his incredible adventure by trading his two pistols to some friendly Indians for the "hine pards of a dog." He wrote: "i ead one of for supper and the other breakfast." Not many wanted to believe White's tale, least of all Major John Wesley Powell, who was still planning his maiden canyon voyage. To descend the Big Cañon alone, as the thirty-year-old White modestly claimed, he would have needed to run—and survive—more than 150 rapids, interspersed with whirlpools and violent eddies, in the span of 277 miles.

White was cast out as a virtual heretic by railroad promoter Robert Brewster Stanton in his posthumously published book *Colorado River Controversies* but was embraced as a hero by Thomas F. Dawson in his June 4, 1917, Senate Resolution No. 79, "First Through the Grand Canyon." The White controversy rages to this day. Records exist of at least one similar log rafter. Forced off course, and nearly out of fuel, forty-four-year-old pilot Daniel Reisman landed his single-engine plane near an abandoned uranium mine in southeastern Utah on July 29, 1959. Stranded without emergency food or water, Reisman climbed down to the Colorado River near Hall Creek and, like James White, made a crude log raft by lashing three cottonwood logs together and started floating down the river toward help. Glen Canyon Dam was still under construction, and Reisman later told reporters that while floating down the Colorado River through Glen Canyon, "the raft turned over in rapids a couple of times but it held together." Reisman was rescued three days after his ordeal began by river guide Earl Johnson, before he got his chance to run the Big Cañon.

BY SWIMMING

If you doubt that James White ran the Grand Canyon on a crude log raft, read Bill Beer's book *We Swam the Colorado River*. On April 10, 1955, twenty-six-year-old Beer and his twenty-seven-year-old partner, John Daggett, waded into the Colorado River at Lees Ferry to begin their daring run through the Grand Canyon. Wearing Mae West life preservers, long underwear, rubber shirts, and swim fins, they towed twenty-five days' worth of food and supplies in waterproof black rubber boxes. For the next twenty days, Daggett and Beer battled a raging undammed river, fatigue, and hypothermia until they reached the head of Lava Falls at River Mile 179. In an August 5, 1955, *Collier's* magazine account, "We Swam the Colorado River," Beer wrote: "Firmly grasping the boxes, I pushed into the river and began to drift slowly toward the stormy rapids. Then the current—and I—picked up speed. I looked for the course I had mapped out, but all I could see were big brown waves. Then I dropped fast and hit bottom hard . . . before I could catch my breath, the stream picked me up and began rolling me over and over until I no longer knew which way was up. I just gasped for breath whenever I saw the sky above." On May 5, Daggett and Beer swam ashore at Pierce Ferry, not far from where James White had beached eighty-eight years earlier.

BY WOODEN BOAT

Whether or not Major John Wesley Powell was the first to run the Grand Canyon of the Colorado River, his 1869 river expedition was the most famous, and perhaps the most important, traverse of the Colorado Plateau and Grand Canyon region. Supported by meager funding, and with an allowance of army rations drawn for twenty-five men, Powell's expedition was composed of twelve men who rowed, lined, portaged, and ran four wooden boats through Lodore, Desolation, Cataract, Glen, and Marble Canyons into the "great unknown" of the Grand Canyon. Even if Powell knew that James White had already made it through the Grand Canyon, as Dawson indicated he might have from reading a February 1869 account in the *Rocky Mountain News*, Powell was nevertheless a true explorer, pioneer river runner, and canyoneer. He surveyed the Grand Canyon of the Colorado River by running it twice, the second time in 1872; traversed the Colorado Plateau on horseback with Jacob Hamblin to visit the Shivwits Paiute and Hopi Regions; and, with one arm, scaled the region's majestic cliffs and landforms.

Running a rapid
W. L. S. AND R. A. MULLER; J. W. POWELL

Many river runners and canyoneers would follow the legendary riverine passages of Ti-Yo, White, and Powell, but by 1950, fewer than a hundred people had run the Grand Canyon of the Colorado River—and at least thirty-eight had died trying. Among many river-running firsts, several stand out. Nathaniel Galloway revolutionized river running in 1896, when he turned around in his rowing seat and faced downstream to pilot his boat down the Colorado River from Green River, Utah, to Lees Ferry, and again in 1897, when he and trapper William Richmond rowed through the Grand Canyon to Needles, "mainly for the hell of it." In 1927, Clyde Eddy was the first—and probably last—boatman to take a bear cub through the Grand Canyon, and in 1937, Buzz Holstrom became the first—but not the last—to make a solo trip through the canyon. In 1951, brothers Jim and Bob Riggs made the first speed run from Lees Ferry to Pierce Ferry when they rowed through the Grand Canyon in two and a half days. Their record was shattered in 1983. Running historic floodwaters peaking at 92,000 cfs, Kenton Grua, Rudi Petschek, and Steve Reynolds survived a nighttime run of—and flip in—the Crystal Hole and rowed through the Grand Canyon in thirty-seven hours!

BY KAYAK

The thirty-seven-hour run was not the only "hair boating" seen on the Colorado River or its tributaries. Kayakers are in a class of whitewater boatmen by themselves. According to Fletcher Anderson and Ann Hopkinson's *Rivers of the Southwest: A Boaters' Guide to the Rivers of Colorado, New Mexico, Utah, and Arizona*, Walter Kirschbaum made the first solo run of the Black Canyon of the Gunnison in 1961 or 1962. Kirschbaum's run wasn't repeated until 1975, when Ron Mason, Filip Sokol, Bill Clark, and Tom Ruwitch paddled the daunting stretch of the Gunnison River that drops 75 feet per mile—nine times steeper than the Colorado River in the Grand Canyon.

No stranger to frothing cataracts, Grand Canyon boatman Brad Dimock kayaked Quartzite Falls on the Upper Salt River twice before eight "ecoterrorists" pleaded guilty to blowing up the Class VI falls with 154 pounds of explosives in 1993. Dimock also made

Climbing with Major Powell
J. W. POWELL

the first descent of the Paria River with Tim Cooper, and in 1976, he and Cooper made the first descent of the 57-mile-long Little Colorado River Gorge. In a riveting *Mountain Gazette* account of their run, "An Exploration of the Little Colorado River Gorge," Tim Cooper wrote of the hazards the expert kayakers encountered: "The rapid continues, careening off one wall, then the other, dividing into channels, foaming and gnashing over more boulders than there is time to count. I can't stop to consider which way to turn or what channel to take. For perhaps half a mile there is only time to stroke and turn, paddle and draw. I finally arrive in calm water with my heart pounding like someone is beating on my sternum with a mallet.

*Grand Canyon climber Dave Ganci negotiates a jump on the 3,512-foot
summit of Diamond Peak, one of the many third-, fourth-, and fifth-class
buttes, peaks, and temples that lure veteran canyoneers to climb the
"summits below the rim."*

Brad paddles up and looks me straight in the eye. He says the first
dead serious thing I've heard him say in several years. 'We could
drown.'" Fortunately, they did not.

BY CLIMBING

Four Arizonans made the first ascent of Colorado's Painted Wall in
the Black Canyon of the Gunnison National Monument in 1973. Led
by Eiger and Troll Wall veteran and alpine climber Rusty Bailie, the
party endured nine days of desperate climbing to make the first
ascent of the 2,000-foot-high Dragon Route.

Climbing throughout the Great Southwest's canyon country
was not limited to such imposing walls. The totems, towers, and
regal landforms of the Navajo Reservation region of the Colorado
Plateau began luring climbers during the late 1930s, and by 1959,
first ascents had been made of the Totem Pole, Spider Rock,
Agathla, and Shiprock—often against tribal beliefs. None, however,

lured climbers or presented the climbing and route-finding difficulties of Shiprock, known to traditional Navajo as *Tse Bit'a'i* ("Winged Rock"). A four-man Sierra Club party—David Brower, John Dyer, Raffi Bedayan, and Bestor Robinson—spent three and a half days climbing the sacred landmark in 1939.

Almost three decades earlier, California topographer Donald McClain made the first recorded ascent of 10,154-foot Picacho del Diablo. Just to reach the mouth of Cañon del Diablo in the remote reaches of northern Baja, McClain traveled by skiff from below Yuma, Arizona, across the Sea of Cortés to San Felipe. From the Mexican gulf port, McClain trekked west across the barren playas and *bajadas* and, in a truly inspirational bit of route finding and climbing, made the first ascent of the Baja Peninsula's highest and most rugged mountain range in 1911.

McClain's ascent, and the host of legendary ascents that followed by other climbers in Canyonlands, Fisher Towers, Arches, and elsewhere throughout the canyon country of the Great Southwest, constitute a vibrant and engaging history that is beyond the scope of this book. For the most part, however, these ascents were limited to summits above the horizon line. It wasn't until Harvey Butchart arrived on the scene in 1945 that climbers really began exploring the possibilities of climbing *in* the Grand Canyon—what Butchart called "the summits below the rim," and what Arizona rock climber Larry Trieber later equated with climbing in a "great inverted mountain range." Where the Anasazi left off, Butchart picked up—climbing to the summits of eighty-three buttes and temples, either alone or with others, fifty being recorded as first ascents. Although Butchart's ascents required keen route finding and endurance, they were for the most part limited to third- and fourth-class climbing. Nonetheless, his explorations and route descriptions laid the foundation for the rock climbers who followed in his footsteps. Among them were Phoenix climbers Dave Ganci and Rick Tidrick; their first ascent of Zoroaster Temple was responsible for cracking the nut of fifth-class climbing on the Grand Canyon's enticing Coconino Sandstone temples. Equipped with marginal supplies of food and water to cross the inner canyon desert from the South Rim, Ganci and Tidrick climbed the Northeast Arête of Zoroaster Temple on September 23, 1958.

BY AIR

Seemingly cut from the same cloth as rock climbers, pilots began barnstorming canyon country not long after the introduction of single-engine planes in the American West. Pilots patrolling the border for the Army Air Service were shooting it out with horseback bandits and smugglers in the canyons of the Big Bend region as early as 1919; that's when Lieutenants F. S. Estill and R. H. Cooper, flying a single-engine DeHavilland called a "flying coffin," gunned down Jesús Rentería and his white horse as he shot it out with them from the back of his mount. In 1922, Commander R. V. Thomas of the British Royal Flying Corps made the first landing and takeoff in the Grand Canyon after he landed his single-engine Thomas Special in a cloud of dust on the Tonto Formation near Plateau Point. The most incredible aerial canyon passage, however, took place in 1944, when three aviators were ordered to bail out over the Grand Canyon after their B-24 developed engine trouble while flying from Tonapah, Nevada, to Tucson, Arizona. After the trio's rescue nine days later, Second Lieutenant Goldblum described to reporters the experience of hurtling through the black wind from 20,000 feet at two in the morning.

> Goldblum said he saw the lights of a town as he came down, which he later learned was Williams. "I watched those lights hoping they would help me with my directions when I landed. Suddenly they blanked out completely as if someone had drawn a blind over them." That, he reasoned later, was when he went over the Grand Canyon rim, and started what is probably the fastest descent ever taken into the huge abyss. . . . Dropping in the night into the canyon, Goldblum jolted to a stop on a narrow ledge. His parachute had caught on rocks overhead. He remained practically motionless until sunrise when he surveyed his position. Nearly 1,200 feet below him was the turbulent Colorado River. From his three-foot ledge, he hoisted himself on his shroud lines to the security of the broader [Tonto] pateau [sic].

6

CANYONEERING

EXPLORING THE WORLD
BENEATH THE HORIZON LINE

If national park visitation figures are any indication, the most popular mode of travel for visiting canyon country is motorized transportation. By the end of 1999, more than five million tourists will have visited Grand Canyon National Park by bus, pickup truck, automobile, train, tour plane, and helicopter. Whether you're a rim-bound tourist aspiring to explore the world below the horizon line or a veteran canyoneer, unless you live with canyon-dwelling Tarahumara, Havasupai, or Navajo, you will undoubtedly drive to the trailhead, river trip put-in, or disembarkation point for your canyon adventure.

That's not to say that you can't explore canyon country by vehicle—it's just not the focus of this book. You can drive to the bottom of the Grand Canyon along the historic route of the Farley Stagecoach Trail, as Los Angeles motorist Byron L. Graves first did sometime before 1910. In an early edition of the *Ford Times,* the Angeleno was described as having nerves of steel for challenging the great abyss from the seat of a Ford: "Never since the creation of the Grand Canyon has there been an automobile in the depths of this historic gorge. Never has there been a driver who cared to risk the dangers of the precipitous descent over rocky passes, knowing full well that the mere slip of a wheel meant a headlong plunge to the

*Canyoneer
Dick Yetman
opts for car
touring at
Lees Ferry,
Arizona.*

rocky bottom of the Canyon." Graves and his companion, Chester Lawrence, made the first descent of the Grand Canyon by automobile in seven hours via what would later become known as the Diamond Creek Road, but not without the use of dynamite to blow trails around boulders and water bags covering their gas tank to keep it from exploding in the sizzling heat.

Canyon car touring is not limited to the Grand Canyon; in fact, there are few national parks in canyon country you can't drive through. South of the border, you can drive on pavement to the headwaters of Cascada de Basaseachic, the most spectacular waterfall in the Barranca del Cobre region; or you can drive from the forested highlands of Creel, Chihuahua, down a steep, winding, dusty track to the bottom of the Barranca de Batopilas.

Few ardent canyoneers, however, limit their explorations to the sweat-stained seat of a well-worn pickup. Most go by boat or anything else that will float: from kayaks to bus-sized motor rigs, from wooden dories to neoprene rafts, from aluminum canoes to inner tubes. One of the all-time life adventures is a two-week-long whitewater trip through the Grand Canyon. If you don't have the expertise to row a private trip through the Grand Canyon, or monastic patience to wait several years for an official river permit, you can book passage with a professional outfitter. But go with one that offers paddle trips; that way, you actually get to earn your nightly ration of boxed wine by paddling and navigating the same legendary big drops that tested Major Powell and drove James White to eat half a dog. If you don't have the time or the money for a Grand Canyon trip, it's far easier to get together a group of friends or business associates, drive south to the Mexican border, rent canoes, and paddle the border canyons of Big Bend National Park.

Like river running, climbing is another thrilling way to explore canyon country. However, since there is a proliferation of how-to manuals and guidebooks that thoroughly address rock climbing, kayaking, and white-water rafting, this chapter highlights canyoneering by foot, one-man raft, and rope.

TRAINING

How did Native Americans train for canyon travel? They didn't "train" per se. Cultures as diverse as the Tarahumara of the Western Sierra Madre and the Southern Paiute of the Grand Canyon revolved around all aspects of canyon life: shivering around communal fires under animal-skin robes; running down rabbits and deer; tending marginal plots of corn, beans, and squash; and traveling long distances on foot for trade and ceremony.

The Tarahumara begin training early for the rigors of travel and day-to-day living in the barrancas *of Mexico's Sierra Madre Occidental.*

Modern man, in contrast, while pioneering the frontiers of science, industry, and technology, has slid down the greased pole of evolution and, for the most part, become a physically underworked, overfed, stressed-out slave to the interstate and the Internet. He no longer runs down supper but sends his wife to the supermarket to buy red meat shrink-wrapped in plastic. He no longer shivers around a bivouac fire but stares wistfully into the fireplace, cradling a hot toddy and his honey while wrapped in a down comforter. He no longer runs a hundred miles to trade but drives his family to theme-park malls, lured by tropical cheeseburgers served by colorfully costumed denizens of the Rain Forest Café.

A creature of comfort, modern man must train. Even those who do physically demanding work, such as bricklayers, construction workers, steelworkers, and roofers, still need to train their legs. But let's assume that you're a desk-bound, city-dwelling flatlander living at or near sea level, with little or no canyoneering experience—as many New Yorkers were before they headed west during the 1800s and became infamous mountain men, gunfighters, and scoundrels. The following training advice is based on that hypothesis. If you're an experienced and fit wilderness foot traveler, all the better; you'll know how to gauge your own training regimen based on the following examples.

"But I'm a runner," you say. Running around New York's Central Park Reservoir near sea level on a crisp, fall day is great for establishing an aerobic base; it may also be good for burning off last night's cocktail hour, closing a deal, or cranking out some record splits, but it doesn't simulate the physical, mental, and environmental conditions of trekking 14 miles and climbing 8,000 vertical feet up Cañon del Diablo to the 10,154-foot summit of Picacho del Diablo during the late spring. Nor does it simulate trekking in and out of the Grand Canyon during the hallucinogenic summer heat—when most people insist on going—or rappelling, swimming, and trekking the slot canyons of the Colorado Plateau. In training for canyoneering, you need to simulate the distance of your journey, the duration, the vertical elevation gain and loss, the climate, and other environmental factors. For example, does your proposed route follow a maintained rim-to-river trail, such as those forged in the Grand Canyon? Or does it involve cross-country travel, boulder hopping, swimming plunge pools, and rappelling? You can prepare for most varieties of canyoneering either by training near where you live or taking a series of canyon adventures that build on one another.

Let's assume that you're a city dweller living far removed from canyon country with plans to enter the Great Unknown in two to three months. Let's look at what it takes physically to make one of the easiest canyon journeys and build up to the more difficult.

DESERT CANYONS

The ancestral land of the Aravaipa Apache, Arizona's Aravaipa Canyon hosts one of the only free-flowing creeks in the Sonoran Desert; as such, it attracts desert and canyon lovers from throughout the United States. In preparing for an overnight spring hike down the length of Aravaipa Canyon, you should train for the rigors of carrying a 25-pound pack on a 12-mile trek. Although the Aravaipa Canyon trek involves a negligible elevation gain and loss, it entails frequent creek crossings in knee-deep water, trudging in wet shoes and socks through coarse sand and gravel, and exposure to a glaring Arizona sun in a warm, dry environment. Going back to Central Park, or if you live elsewhere near sea level, such as San

Aerial view of the ancestral land of the canyon-dwelling Aravaipa Apache, Aravaipa Canyon, Arizona.

Francisco, Dallas, Phoenix, or Chicago, running or walking 3 to 5 miles a day three times a week for six weeks before your canyon adventure will strengthen your leg muscles, establish an aerobic base, and perhaps burn off the bulge. But you should inure yourself further by embarking on six weekend training outings of two consecutive 5- to 6-mile days carrying the same pack weight you plan to carry through Aravaipa Canyon. Nothing short of soaking your feet in a pailful of piranha, however, will prepare you for walking in wet shoes and socks filled with abrasive sand and gravel.

Some old wives' tales tell of being able to toughen your feet by soaking them in salt water. I've found such measures to be a remedy for sore feet *after* rugged canyon journeys. There's no getting around it: You need to condition your feet by walking, running, or hiking to prepare them for the rigors of canyoneering. Just as importantly, make sure that your footwear is well broken in before you leave the canyon rim, or those new boots may have you hobbling with bloody blisters.

SLOT CANYONS

The ancestral land of the Kaibab and Kaiparowits bands of Southern Paiute, the deep incised meanders formed by Buckskin Gulch and Paria Canyon, offer one of the most beautiful canyon journeys in the Great Southwest. They attract a mélange of canyoneers, from solo walkers in search of their destiny to camo-faced Boy Scout troops itching to gun down their adolescent demons. Like Aravaipa Canyon, the Buckskin Gulch–Paria Canyon loop trek also involves a negligible elevation gain and loss, but it is 7 miles longer. So if you plan to travel that 19 miles in two days, as most canyoneers do, you should maintain your base of running or walking 3 to 5 miles a day three times a week for six weeks, but increase your six weekend outings to two consecutive 10-mile days carrying the same pack weight you plan to lug through Paria Narrows. A spectacular crack in the earth's crust, Buckskin Gulch is choked with flash-flood debris such as logjams, boulders, and pools of stagnant water, so in addition to preparing for the rigors of walking and skating around dead coyotes on slick, shoe-sucking mud, you should do some upper-body training to get ready for the rigors of lowering packs and climbing over logjams and boulders.

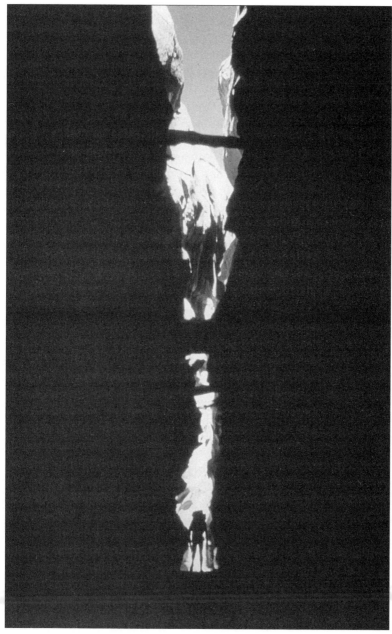

A canyoneer threads the deep slot canyon of Buckskin Gulch, Utah.

EXPLORING CANYON COUNTRY BY ROPE: THE ESSENTIALS

By their very nature, most canyon routes follow prehistoric, historic, and modern routes of travel; thus, it is the exception, not the norm, when a rope is required. Most veteran canyoneers try to avoid situations that require the use of ropes, because it is usually easier to change your route and skirt a perilous drop-off than to pack in a cumbersome rope, seat harness, carabiners, helmet, and the like. Nonetheless, as evidenced by the Hopi salt expeditions, ropes were sometimes required to descend into canyons long before the advent of modern perlon ropes. The most common type of rope work you're likely to use in canyon country is a hand line.

HAND LINES

Hand lines are used to negotiate chockstones such as those wedged into the enclosed meanders of Buckskin Gulch, descend into fissures such as Antelope Canyon, and penetrate the headwaters of narrows such as Deer Creek Falls in the Grand Canyon. They are also used to gain access into the mouths of canyons from below. Before it was cut down because of a series of tragic accidents, a looped hand line enabled river runners to climb the pouroff, or overhang, into the mouth of Olo Canyon from the Colorado River; a steel cable is still used to negotiate the slick walls in the lower reaches of the Cañon del Diablo in the Sierra San Pedro Mártir of Baja California Norte. Along such established routes of travel, you will generally find these hand lines in place. However, if your firsthand information or a reliable guidebook indicates that they are not in place, you will have to carry your own coil of rope to safeguard passage over that tricky section of rock. The length of rope needed depends on the height of the obstacle, which you can determine from reliable sources before you go. Gold line is a popular choice because of its ability to withstand abrasion. Descending or climbing a dangling hand line with a cumbersome pack can be

A river runner ascends the difficult hand line that once provided access into the mouth of Olo Canyon from the Colorado River.

dangerous, and you may find it easier and safer to lower or raise your pack with your hand line. If you don't need to carry a rope, you can save on space and weight by using parachute shroud line to lower and raise your pack on short hauls of 20 to 30 feet.

RAPPELLING

Although a small number of highly skilled and conditioned canyoneers use rappelling extensively for exploring the technical slot canyons of southeastern Utah, the vast majority of veteran canyoneers use rappelling only when they can't find an alternative route that allows them to safely scramble into a canyon or if there is no other way to bypass obstacles such as chockstones or boulders, which are characteristically wedged into slot canyons and the heads of narrows. Rappelling is more commonly used by rock climbers in canyon country to reach isolated fingers of rock, such as 6,800-foot Comanche Point

A climber rappels over the edge of Comanche Point on the South Rim of the Grand Canyon to reach the base of 6,800-foot Comanche Point Pinnacle.

Pinnacle off the South Rim of the Grand Canyon, or to descend from the lofty summits of temples, towers, and buttes. But unless you're enrolled in a canyoneering field course such as Outward Bound's month-long Canyonlands' program or are being taught on site by a skilled and knowledgeable companion, I do not advise you to learn how to rappel in canyon country. This is a technical and often dangerous aspect of rock climbing and mountaineering that you should learn and master before you try exploring a technical slot canyon that demands the skill of rock climber, the stamina of an athlete, and the tolerance for thirst of a desert rat.

The characteristics of rappelling in canyon country, however, distinguish it from rappelling down slick, even overhanging walls after rock climbing. Cactus and brush can obstruct natural rappel anchors such as trees and boulders, and loose rock and rubble can pose hazards once you've begun your rappel if they become dislodged. Rappelling over a chockstone to gain access into a narrow canyon can prove tricky for both novice and experienced canyoneers because these huge, awkward boulders, lodged into a narrow pinch of walls, are undercut and are frequently running with water. To keep from slipping and getting banged up during your rappel, you need to place your feet wide apart, with knees bent, and lean way back in your rappel harness as you walk backward over the lip of the chockstone. Finally, and perhaps most critically, if your landing zone is a plunge pool, the first person to rappel into the water needs to carry his inflated raft on a short cord dangling behind him so that he can sit in it when he's reached water level. Once his rappel is complete, the lead rappeller should paddle out of the fall line and have the next person lower his or her raft so that the leader can position it, and so on for the next canyoneer.

BELAYING

Belaying is a form of protecting another climber, in this case a canyoneer, with a rope while climbing and rappelling. Like rappelling, belaying is a skill that you should also learn before you head out to canyon country if your proposed route involves more than simple hiking, trekking, or scrambling. If there is ever any doubt about negotiating a tricky section of rock (see Class System, below), an exposed ledge, or a hand line, and you can't safely spot your companions with your hands, take the time to belay them. And always belay one another during rappels.

CLASS SYSTEM

Reportedly developed by the Sierra Club during the 1930s, the following system of classes has been used to describe the difficulty of and equipment needs for backcountry travel and climbing. Source: Michael Loughman, *Learning to Rock Climb* (San Francisco: Sierra Club Books, 1981).

Class	Equipment and Technique
1	Walking. No special equipment or technique.
2	Scrambling. Proper shoes advisable. Hands may be needed for balance.
3	Climbing. A rope should be available for [belaying] inexperienced climbers.
4	Exposed climbing (a fall could be fatal). A rope and belays are advisable. Belay anchors may be needed.
5	Difficult free climbing. Protection anchors for the leader are advisable. [Class 5 is now delineated by the decimal system, developed at Tahquitz Rock during the 1950s, for grading rock climbing difficulties 5.1 through 5.13.]
6	Aided climbing. The rope and anchors are used for assistance in moving upward.

MOGOLLON RIM CANYONS

The ancestral land of the northeastern Yavapai and the Tonto band of Western Apache, the canyons of the Mogollon Rim bridge the threshold between the forested highlands of the Colorado Plateau and the Sonoran Desert lowlands of the Basin and Range; they attract experienced canyoneers versed in an array of canyoneering skills. One of the many factors that distinguishes exploring the canyons of the Mogollon Rim, such as the West Fork of Oak Creek, Wet Beaver Creek, West Clear Creek, and Salome Creek, from desert canyons such as Aravaipa Creek and slot canyons such as Buckskin Gulch is the succession of plunge pools that need to be crossed by swimming, floating, or paddling. In training for the 14-mile trek down the length of Wet Beaver Creek, you should continue to run or walk 3 to 5 miles a day, three times a week for six weeks, and maintain your six weekend outings of two consecutive 7- to 10-mile days carrying the same pack weight you plan to haul down Wet Beaver Creek. You should also do some upper-body work to prepare for the physical rigors of either rappelling with a pack or down-climbing seven abrupt drop-offs at the head of Wet Beaver Creek.

Three other factors enter the Wet Beaver Creek picture you didn't experience in either Aravaipa Canyon or Paria Canyon:

Footing. Slick, mossy boulders limit walking and stumbling to 1 mile an hour.

Elevation Loss. Top to bottom, Wet Beaver Creek drops 2,300 vertical feet.

Plunge Pools. Two dozen cold plunge pools (25 to 75 yards long) need to be crossed.

You can train for the slick boulders by doing your weekend hikes along creek bottoms and talus slopes, and the elevation loss can be simulated during weekend hill or mountain hikes and by walking or running stadium steps at the local high school on the weekdays, but the plunge pools are another story. If you're fit enough to carry the additional weight of a one-man raft, you can paddle across each plunge pool. You can train for carrying the extra weight by lugging the raft through the woods on your weekend hikes—just be prepared for strange stares if you pack it around inflated. And before you head out to canyon country, you should actually practice paddling in a swimming pool—the way Bill Beer and John Daggett did before their epic swim—so you have a sense of what it takes to paddle a tiny raft loaded with a heavy pack. For the sake of expediency, some canyoneers, myself included, pack their gear in a waterproof river bag fitted with shoulder straps and swim each plunge pool, paddling the bag in front of them while hanging on. However, unless you're a strong swimmer or a triathlete, you should train for swimming these plunge pools by including a minimum of two half-mile pool sessions a week for six weeks on the days you're not doing your training runs or walks or stadium steps.

A canyoneer uses a military surplus "black bag" and an inflatable U.S. Diver's life vest to swim the cold, deep plunge pools of the West Fork of Oak Creek, Arizona.

STAIRSTEP CANYONS

The ancestral land of the Hualapai, Havasupai, Southern Paiute, Hopi, and Navajo, the Grand Canyon of the Colorado River lures tens of thousands of hikers and adventurers from around the globe each year, from high-heeled neophytes to Outward Bound expeditions. In training for a 16- to 22-mile roundtrip rim-to-river hike in

EXPLORING CANYON COUNTRY BY RAFT

For the most part, a one-man raft is used to cross the deep, cold plunge pools of canyons such as Wet Beaver Creek, West Clear Creek, and other water-choked corridors. However, there is a labyrinth of a hundred-odd tributary canyons that once drained into the Escalante River, San Juan River, and Colorado River arms of Glen, Narrow, and Cataract Canyons that can still be explored by one-man raft. Inundated by 186-mile-long Lake Powell and rimmed by 1,900 miles of its shoreline, most of these once tranquil canyons are now probed by all manner of watercraft ranging from houseboats, power boats, and jet skis to sea kayaks. To escape the din of summer crowds, however, you can explore some of the area's seldom-visited canyons in the heart of Anasazi country by driving, packing, or hiking in to their headwaters from above. Once you've reached your disembarkation point, you can use a one-man raft to explore these canyon recesses; you'll also want to include a life vest, internal framed pack, or a dry bag fitted with shoulder straps, and your personal war chest of food and camping gear (see Gear Checklist on page 135).

the Grand Canyon, you should continue to run or walk 3 to 5 miles a day, three times a week for six weeks and increase your six weekend outings to two consecutive 8- to 11-mile days carrying the same pack weight you plan to hump in and out of the Grand Canyon. The average 5,000-vertical-foot elevation loss, and 5,000-vertical-foot elevation gain, entailed in rim-to-river hiking is a different beast; few regimens other than climbing mountains with an equivalent elevation gain and loss will simulate the effect of descending into and climbing out of the Grand Canyon. The vast majority of Americans, however, do not live within the immediate vicinity of a mountain with an elevation gain and loss of a vertical mile, so you will probably have to experiment. Canyoneers living in the Sonoran Desert lowlands of Phoenix, Arizona, for example, can often be seen training for Grand Canyon treks by climbing up and down Squaw

Peak with a pack; the 1.1-mile Squaw Peak Trail climbs over 1,000 vertical feet, and by hiking up and down the steep, rocky trail two to three times back-to-back, the rigors of descending halfway into and climbing halfway out of the Grand Canyon can be simulated. If you are a stone flatlander living in Kansas, there are other ways to simulate the training effects of elevation gain and loss: running or walking stadium steps at the local high school or college track, climbing the stairwells of high-rises, and using stair-climbing machines. You will have to start slowly and experiment until you've worked up to the equivalent of climbing 1,000 vertical feet in an hour. Once you've accomplished that, you can increase your workouts until you're simulating the elevation loss and gain of your forthcoming canyon adventure.

Several other pivotal factors enter the Grand Canyon picture. Hiking from the North or South Rim down to the Colorado River and back is the reverse of mountain climbing. First you hammer your knees and thighs by descending a steep vertical mile into one of the Seven Natural Wonders of the World; then you lay over a day next to a creek to lick your wounds, bandage your feet, and swat flies. Still stiff and sore from the descent, you turn around on day three and are faced with a daunting mountain to climb before you get home. But the higher you climb, the more fatigued you become, not only from the rigors of the trek but also from the increase in altitude from 2,450 feet to 7,260 or 8,199 feet or more above sea level.

Heat. Even in ideal weather conditions, the physical rigors of hiking a maintained trail in and out of the Grand Canyon can tax trained athletes. The vast majority of canyon hikers and trekkers, however, do not go during the pleasant days of spring or fall; they go during vacation time in the blistering heat of summer. As dangerous as trekking the grim, relatively level track of the Camino del Diablo is during the searing heat of summer, it does not compare with the rigors of climbing through the scorching black walls of the Inner Gorge on a cloudless June day, carrying a heavy pack loaded with enough water to get you back to the South Rim alive. Your body, already tired from the hike in, is being stressed by the steep climb, the linear distance, dehydration, and the heat. Remember

*Climbing out of
the Grand Canyon*
KING; J. W. POWELL

how C. Hart Merriam was punished by the heat in the Painted Desert? If you don't have the good fortune of living and training in one of the Southwest's deserts and you insist on trekking into the Grand Canyon in midsummer, or elsewhere in canyon country this side of the lofty reaches of the Western Sierra Madre, you might try simulating the heat by wearing cotton sweats during your weekly training runs or walks and on your weekend hikes. But check with your physician first.

Altitude. In trekking out of the Grand Canyon—or the Barranca del Cobre, for that matter—your time at altitudes above 5,000 feet will probably be limited to the two to three hours it takes you to climb from that level out to the rim. But if they come at the end of your rim-to-river trek, these may be the most difficult miles on your canyon journey. So if you're driving from sea level to the Grand Canyon or the Barranca del Cobre region, you should consider spending a day hiking around the rim country before your canyon trek to get a sense of what physical exertion feels like at altitudes above 5,000 feet, where many people first begin to feel the effects of the decreased oxygen.

Nonmaintained Trails. Let's assume that you're not one of the tens of thousands of hikers who'll be trekking one of the Grand Canyon's maintained rim-to-river trails. You've got some Canyon experience, so you want to try a nonmaintained trail such as the Nankoweap, Tanner, Hance, or North Bass. If you don't have the luxury of living near the Grand Canyon, you should do some of your weekend hikes on nonmaintained trails in your area to simulate the rigors of cross-country trekking and to practice your route-finding skills.

In training for using nonmaintained trails and routes, you should follow the same training regimen previously outlined for hiking maintained trails. Equally important is to gain firsthand experience, knowledge, and conditioning by hiking maintained canyon trails before moving on to the challenges of hiking, trekking, and scrambling along nonmaintained trails and routes. Training, safety, water sources, and proper gear (see Gear Checklist on page 135) are even more important considerations on such routes because they are, by nature, far off the heavily beaten path where other canyoneers, hikers, and backcountry ranger patrols might otherwise be able to assist you during an emergency.

Rim-to-Rim-to-Rim Routes and Trails. You're a 5.11 rock climber and you want to do a new route on Buddha or Zoroaster Temple, or you're an explorer and you want to follow the historic route of cartographer François Emile Matthes down the South Bass Trail, across the Colorado River, and up the North Bass Trail to the North Rim, where you'll camp for a night before returning by the same route. Although the linear distance differs somewhat for both scenarios, the total elevation gain and loss is essentially double that of the average rim-to-river Grand Canyon trek: 10,000 vertical feet each way. Even if your rim-to-rim-to-rim route takes the Bright Angel and North Kaibab Trails, as many cross-canyon hikers opt to do, in one of your training outings you need to simulate the equivalent of traveling 40 miles in four days with an elevation loss and gain of 10,000 vertical feet each way.

Inner Canyon Routes and Tributary Gorges. Canyoneering in the Grand Canyon and Colorado Plateau region is not limited to

Dave Ganci catches his breath on the difficult third class approach from the South Rim of the Grand Canyon to the base of Zoroaster Temple.

rim-to-river trails and rim-to-rim-to-rim routes. Inner canyon routes such as the nonmaintained, 72-mile-long Tonto Trail course east to west through the heart of the Grand Canyon; if you access Tonto Trail on the east end via the Grandview Trail and follow the length of it west to the South Bass Trail, you will travel over 80 miles. If you're interested in trekking 60 miles down the length of Kanab Creek canyon along the historic route of the gold rush, you need to add another 20 miles, and a 5,166-vertical-foot ascent, to climb out of the Grand Canyon via the Colorado River and the Deer Creek and Thunder River Trails. If you want to trek 57 miles down the length of the Little Colorado River Gorge, where few historic or modern canyoneers have ventured, you need to add another 18 miles, and a 4,660-vertical-foot ascent, to climb out of the Grand Canyon via the Beamer and Tanner Trails. These three multiday treks average 80 miles each. On the conservative side, plan on trekking 2 miles an hour for eight to ten hours a day. That's 16 to 20 miles a day for four to five days that you need to simulate in one of your training outings—perhaps on a four-day weekend.

MOUNTAIN CANYONS

The ancestral land of the Kiliwa, Akwa'ala, Ñakipa, and Juigrepa, the stone canyons of the Sierra San Pedro Mártir normally attract only the hardiest and most experienced of canyoneers. But let's assume that you've got a couple of Grand Canyon treks under your belt and you're feeling your oats. You're tired of the crowds at Phantom Ranch, and you heard the siren call of the Forgotten Peninsula. Foot for foot and mile for mile, few canyon journeys in the Great Southwest are as rugged and difficult as the trek up Cañon del Diablo to the 10,154-foot summit of Picacho del Diablo. In the span of 14 miles, you will boulder hop, scramble, and climb more than 8,000 vertical feet—one way. But the numbers don't tell the whole story. There is no trail up the boulder-choked depths of Cañon del Diablo. And there are few ways to simulate the rigors of this journey other than by embarking on a series of other canyon adventures that build up to an ascent of Picacho del Diablo. Nobody lives here—airliners don't even fly overhead—so nobody's going to do a grid search for you with choppers, trackers, infrared sensors, and bloodhounds, the way they might in the Grand Canyon; and no indigenous canyon dweller will mysteriously appear out of nowhere to offer you a gourdful of water or pinole the way they might if you got lost in the Barranca del Cobre region.

BEFORE YOU GO

Mental Preparation. If you're a city dweller accustomed to having throngs of people around you or catering to your every beck and call, you should log an equivalent amount of wilderness time— perhaps during your weekend training outings—either alone or with companions to prepare for the solace, or isolation, of exploring remote, seldom-visited canyons such as Cañon del Diablo, Escalante Creek, and the Galiuro Mountains' Redfield Canyon.

Itinerary and Route Description. Even the most experienced canyoneers can sprain an ankle, get bitten by a scorpion, or fall ill in the wilderness. Before you go, make a photocopy of your itinerary and give it to someone you trust with your life. Also give that person a road map highlighted with your route to your disembarkation point and topographical maps highlighted with your proposed itinerary, campsites, and route of travel. Just don't deviate from your route or itinerary once you're in canyon country. That way, if you're a no-show for dinner on Sunday or work on Monday morning, rescuers will have a specific area to begin searching during those first precious hours when you're still conscious enough to snivel beneath a boulder.

TRAVELING ESSENTIALS

If you live in the New West, you see them everywhere: four-wheel-drive trucks and sport utility vehicles booted with shiny black off-road tires and nary a scratch on their doors. Those are two dead giveaways that their owners never drive them off the pavement and use them for what they were intended. In fact, the closest most of these vehicles get to "Ford tough country" is the parking lot of the IMAX theater or the Rain Forest Café—which brings us to the subject of gear. Do you really need a $30,000 four-wheel-drive vehicle to reach the disembarkation point for your canyon adventure, or would a taxi or beat-up pickup do the job just as well? This section sticks to the rudiments of what you actually need for canyoneering, not what you may be talked into buying at the local automall or backpacking boutique.

Peek into the closet of the average Grand Canyon backpacker, and you will see what amounts to a mother lode of high-tech gear that sits idle all but one or two weeks of the year; nearly every item cost the equivalent of a month's wages or more in the Barranca del Cobre region, and none of it shows much sign of natural wear and tear: leather boots, nylon pack, down sleeping bag, stormproof tent, butane stove, stainless steel pots and pans, cappuccino maker, wine opener, cheese cutter, water pump, miniature lantern, compass, camera, shortwave radio, binoculars, and a sport utility knife that can disassemble the cargo door of a smoldering Colombian transport plane. It quickly tallies up to more than $1,000. So if you're gearing up for that once-a-year spring or summer hike to Havasupai with a similar stockpile of accoutrements in mind, divide $1,000 by 16 miles and you're looking at over $62 per mile, not including gas, food, and lodging between home and Hualapai Hilltop, and permit fees once you've reached your canyon Shangri-la.

If, on the other hand, you have the good fortune to be invited into the cave or stone dwelling of a Tarahumara, you will see that these ancient canyoneers wear virtually everything they will use to travel throughout Mexico's canyon country, in rain or drought, for the entire year. They are dressed in handmade leather huarache sandals with tire-tread soles; a breechcloth and handwoven shirt; a headband or Mexican cowboy hat; a cloth sling for carrying food such as pinole, corn tortillas, and tamales; and an old wool blanket for cold weather and sleeping.

Traveling among indigenous, mestizo, and Mexican canyon dwellers of the Southwest borderlands and Western Sierra Madre has a way of changing your perspective on what is essential for backcountry travel and living and what is not. The following suggestions are based on that perspective and years of honing my own canyon gear down to the basics. If, however, you want to throw a cell phone, global positioning system, power notebook, and sat-com

A Tarahumara dressed and equipped for canyoneering in the Barranca de Batopilas.

into your war chest of gear so schoolchildren in Toledo, Ohio, can watch your group on the Internet celebrate its first canyon trek at the Phantom Ranch beer hall, good humping!

GEAR FOR DAY TRIPS

You can easily hike Aravaipa Canyon end to end in a day, but the car shuttle is so long that some parties divide their group in two, hike through from opposite ends, swap car keys in the middle, and rendezvous at a Mexican restaurant later that night to switch vehicles. Or you can hike out and back midway through Aravaipa Canyon from one end or the other. For either scenario, you don't need much more than what you came into this world with. Remember the Tarahumara and James White. Even C. Hart Merriam's overnight Grand Canyon trek was outfitted with little more than "some traps + a bag of pancakes + our guns." Footwear for wading through water and walking in coarse sand and gravel varies from sport sandals to running shoes. Most hikers wear shorts, but if you don't have the sinewy, weathered legs of a Tarahumara, you might consider wearing knee-length wool socks for protection from brush. Upper garments? Dress for the weather. Headgear varies from ball caps and tennis hats to headbands and sombreros. Your day pack should include food, water, matches, a knife, a topographical map, and a first-aid kit. My pared-down first-aid kit is a bottle of aspirin, a knife, and a roll of surgical adhesive tape.

This outfit does not need to change significantly for day hiking the Virgin River Narrows end to end during the summer or day hiking Paria Canyon to the Buckskin Gulch confluence and back. If you are headed to Antelope Canyon, however, chances are you will have 70 pounds of photo equipment, a model who's never been west of Manhattan, her stylist, the creative director, your assistant, and a local Navajo guide to warn you that flash-flood danger is up because it's raining.

If you are fit and motivated, you can also trek and swim end to end through canyons such as Wet Beaver Creek in one long, warm summer day. But you should consider adding two essential pieces of equipment: a river bag fitted with nylon straps for carrying your day gear and paddling across plunge pools, and an inflatable diver's life vest for flotation should cold-water immersion fatigue you—and it will.

GEAR FOR OVERNIGHT TRIPS

There are many reasons for camping in canyon country; two of the most frequent considerations, perhaps, are that you simply want to sleep out and howl at the moon, or that it's impractical or impossible to complete your canyon sojourn in a day. Once you go overnight, however, the gear scenario changes: You have to carry extra food, water, and gear to carry the additional weight.

Desert Canyons. In Aravaipa Canyon, you need to dress for the weather and carry a pack large enough to include overnight essentials such as a sleeping bag, a stove (if you don't cook on a fire), the caloric equivalent of three meals, water, a means of purifying water (by chlorinating, boiling, or filtering), a tent fly for rain or shade (if you don't camp beneath rock overhangs), a first-aid kit, and instructions for your fleet-footed Apache scout to wait for you at the trailhead because you want to stay behind and commune with Mother Nature. Since you'll be carrying a heavier load, you may also want

John Annerino bivouacs in the West Fork of Oak Creek during a 750-mile wilderness run from Mexico to Utah.

to wear sturdier footwear than sandals or running shoes, such as a lightweight hiking boot.

Slot Canyons and Mogollon Rim Canyons. Here, as in Aravaipa, you should be prepared, dressed, and outfitted for the terrain and weather and carry the essentials listed above in an internal-framed pack, including the caloric equivalent of two to three meals a day. For a Tarahumara, that averages out to 1,600 calories a day; a dieting American who's not cheating consumes between 2,200 and 2,500 calories a day, and a backpacker humping a bulging pack with all the forbidden fruits and drink he swore off after New Year's will probably force-feed himself 3,500 to 4,000 calories a day. For technical slot canyons, you need to carry a 120- to 150-foot length of 9-mm or 11-mm perlon rope for rappelling and belaying, a seat harness, carabiners, a helmet, nylon slings for rappel and belay anchors, a one-man raft (military surplus or commercial), a waterproof pack, and, I strongly advise, an inflatable dive vest. The handful of canyoneers who explore these canyons in the off-season, between late fall and early spring, wear half- or full-length wet suits for wading and swimming plunge pools they don't paddle across.

Gorges, Stairstep Canyons, and Mountain Canyons. In canyon country, you are generally faced with too much water or not enough water. Access to drinking water in stairstep canyons and mountain canyons can change markedly from access in slot canyons and Mogollon Rim canyons, because oftentimes your route will stray far from water sources. Many examples come immediately to mind: In the Grand Canyon, the Tanner Trail and Nankoweap Trail can be particularly unforgiving for the unprepared. The same holds true—only more so—for the Little Colorado River Gorge. In trekking 57 miles down the length of the Little Colorado River Gorge from Cameron to its confluence with the Colorado River, the best footing is generally encountered during the searing month of June, when mud from the spring runoff has been sun-baked to a hard, firm crust; however, to reach the first reliable water source at Blue Springs 35 miles down-canyon, you need to carry a *minimum* of 3 gallons of water: a gallon for every 10 miles, at 8 1/2 pounds a gallon. When carrying more than 2 gallons of water, I carry a 1-gallon jug in the bottom of my pack and two 1-gallon jugs strapped to the

Canyoneers Bob Farrell (right) and his companion tank up at a deep water pocket during a hot, trailless 3-day journey down the length of Sycamore Canyon, Arizona.

outside of my pack behind my shoulders. Once at Blue Springs, the scenery goes from spectacular to awe inspiring, but the water situation does not improve greatly. Although Blue Springs is *usually* dependable, the water is heavy with carbonates. You can dilute the foul, stomach-wrenching taste by purifying it with a water pump in order to have enough drinking water to cover the remaining 22 miles to the Colorado River. I prefer to mask the taste with powdered electrolyte drinks during the day and by boiling coffee grounds in it for breakfast and my evening meal. Because some "sport drinks" have a high sugar content, they can cause stomach cramps; coffee has also proved to be a diuretic in spite of its ability to get you moving and help convert fat to energy. So if you don't come from the John Wesley Powell school of boiling coffee grounds in bad water, use a water pump. Scarcity of water can also be a problem in Cañon del Diablo, where, as in the Little Colorado River Gorge, you have to be prepared to hump the weight over boulders as you climb 8,000 vertical feet through the glaring heat and icy shadows.

The second most important equipment consideration for exploring gorges, stairstep canyons, and mountain canyons is footwear. You should wear a sturdy, well-broken-in pair of leather boots that offer protection for your feet, support for your ankles, and traction for walking, boulder hopping, and scrambling. Boots with Vibram, or high-carbon rubber, soles that stick to wet rocks are best.

ORIENTATION AND ROUTE FINDING

You've already had an overview of reading landforms and identifying the geological stratigraphy of canyon country in chapters 2 and 4. You can further enhance your knowledge before heading into canyon country by studying the geology guidebooks produced by many different national parks, as well as the multicolor USGS geological maps for the area you plan to visit. The same holds true for identifying the peculiar landforms of canyon country; if you don't live in canyon country, study Hamblin and Murphy's *Grand Canyon Perspectives* and Stokes's *Scenes of the Plateau Lands* (listed in the Bibliography). Carry a compass, know how to use it, and use it

Orientation and route finding
J. Enthoffer, Photoengraving; Clarence E. Dutton

frequently with your topographical map to know where you are, where you've come from, and where you're headed.

Unless you need to shoot a bearing through a dense ponderosa pine forest in someplace like the Kaibab Plateau to reach the head of a little-used descent route, you may not need your compass. In the Great Southwest, the landforms, geology, and other natural orientation points are generally so striking that you can often see where you need to go. However, the details of how your route courses through and around natural barriers that might stand between Point A and Point B can vary widely, and it may require you to be proficient in reading landforms on the horizon line and recognizing and orienting them on your topographical map, and knowing the geological stratigraphy of the canyon you're exploring and how to discern its lines of weakness and best course of travel.

Watercourses. Route finding along watercourses that form natural travel corridors such as Aravaipa Canyon, the Virgin River Narrows, Buckskin Gulch–Paria River, the Little Colorado River Gorge, and the Barranca de Sinforosa, among many, is easy: You will be traveling either upstream or downstream. You will, however, be required to make route-finding decisions as to which is the best way around obstacles such as logjams, boulder slides, cliffs, dead-end ledge systems, and so forth. Route finding becomes more complicated when traveling by foot along watercourses such as the Colorado River in the Grand Canyon, where the route may require you to climb hundreds to 1,000 vertical feet or more through formations such as the Vishnu Group to traverse above barriers along the river's edge. The same holds true for Cañon del Diablo; once you've trekked, boulder-hopped, and scrambled 14 grueling miles upstream to the base of Picacho del Diablo, you still need to be savvy enough to follow the steep third-class route to the summit and back.

Rim-to-River, Inner Canyon, and Cross-Canyon. In trekking rim-to-river along nonmaintained trails or routes, be it the Black Canyon of the Gunnison, the Grand Canyon, or elsewhere, you also need to be familiar with the geological stratigraphy of each canyon and how to follow faint paths and trail markers. The same holds true for inner canyon routes such as the Grand Canyon's 72-mile-long

Canyon in Escalante
H. H. Nichols; J. W. Powell

Canyoneer Richard Nebeker makes his way down the flood-swollen corridor of Buckskin Gulch during a four-day canyon adventure.

Tonto Trail and cross-canyon routes such as the North Rim's Butte Fault and the Barranca del Cobre's Cusaráre to Divisadero trek. Learning how to follow a faint footpath and discern the difference between a canyoneer's route and a bighorn sheep trail comes with practice, and you gain your own knowledge of "sign cutting" by spending hours in the field with your eyes open, your senses attuned to being aware and observant, and your mind focused on the subtle details of the path and its natural line of travel.

SAFETY

Weather and Season. The best season and weather conditions for canyon exploration vary widely throughout the Great Southwest. For example, spring is great for trekking Aravaipa Canyon, the Grand Canyon, the Barranca del Cobre, and the border canyons of the Big Bend, but it is generally still too cold to wade or swim the slot canyons and Mogollon Rim canyons, too wet to trek the Little

Colorado River Gorge, and, unless you're prepared for snow, too cold or icy to summit Picacho del Diablo without adequate gear. June through July, until the onset of summer monsoons, is generally a good time to explore the slot canyons, Mogollon Rim canyons, and other plateau canyons such as Virgin River Narrows and the Black Canyon of the Gunnison, but it's too hot for most people to safely enjoy rim-to-river trekking in the Grand Canyon, Canyon-lands, or the border canyons of Big Bend. July–August monsoon season can prove deadly in the slot canyons and is mostly cold and damp in the Western Sierra Madre.

There are many ways to discern the ideal season and weather in which to explore a particular canyon. You can call or write to the managing agency of a particular area and ask. You can request backcountry information on the area and study it. You can read the natural history books and trail guides on the area. You can watch the Weather Channel. And you can ask an old hand who knows the area firsthand. However, the vagaries of vacation schedules and depersonalized reservation computer systems often preclude canyoneers from visiting popular areas during the ideal time. As a result, if your area's already booked up and you and your compan-ions are locked into visiting, say, the Grand Canyon in June, you may be offered the hellish alternative of making the Nankoweap Canyon death march when you really had your sights set on going trout fishing, by way of Thunder River, at the confluence of Tapeats Creek and the Colorado River.

Escape Routes and Emergency Courses of Action. Know your escape routes and have an emergency course of action thought through before you head out to canyon country. That way, if things go south once you're in canyon country, you'll have a good idea whether your best escape route is to go back the way you came or if there's a shorter, perhaps easier route. The best escape route is generally the way you entered a canyon, because you already have an intimate knowledge of the route; a good guidebook includes this information with its route descriptions. However, if you're certain that a different route will be quicker and safer, you may opt to use it. Only you and your companions can assess the situation and the most effective emergency course of action once you're in the field.

Although some veteran canyoneers prefer to travel alone, they are generally required by national park backcountry ranger offices to leave a detail of their footprints so that park rangers know what to look for if they're no-shows or late checking out. Most canyoneers, however, stick by the safety-in-numbers theory and travel with companions, not only for the camaraderie but also in the event that they need help.

If you or someone in your party gets in a jam, should you sit and pray for help, send a companion out to get help, or initiate a self-rescue? Let's use a sprained ankle as a hypothetical situation. If you're hiking with friends in Aravaipa Canyon and one of you sprains an ankle, you can make a crutch or walking stick out of an agave stalk and assist the injured person out. It will be hard, the miles will be difficult, and you may have to leave precious, unneeded possessions cached behind, but you can do it. The same scenario becomes more complicated if you sprain an ankle in Wet Beaver Creek. If you're beyond the midway point, or the point of no return, you can still get down-canyon and float the plunge pools, but it will be very difficult, and you'll have to steel yourself for the pain, workload, and mental effort. If you're 40 miles into a solo descent of the Little Colorado River Gorge and you sprain an ankle, you can try using your signal mirror if any aircraft are flying overhead, but don't wait forever. Get started crawling toward the Colorado River, where you'll have a better chance of signaling airliners, air tour operators, river runners, and the South Rim vista at Desert View. Spraining an ankle in Cañon del Diablo can be a far more serious situation. Assuming that your companion sprains his ankle and you're too far up-canyon to get him all the way back to the vehicle, you'll need to help him reach a reliable water source. Once you've established a camp for him nearby and provisioned him with an adequate supply of food, drinking water and firewood, until your return, you'll need to make it back to the vehicle without panicking and spraining your own ankle, drive to San Felipe, and call an air ambulance out of San Diego or the helicopter rescue unit based at the Marine Corps Air Station, Yuma.

In the craggy mountain gorges of the Gila Mountains, Arizona, a Navy corpsman directs a rescue training exercise from a litter suspended from a Marine Corps helicopter.

Canyon travelers resting at Elfin Water Pocket
J. W. POWELL

DRINKING WATER

Water Sources. On the Arizona Strip and in Utah's canyon country, water holes are called water pockets; south of Arizona's Gila River in the deserts and mountain canyons bordering the Camino del Diablo, they are called *tinajas* ("rock tanks"); and south of the U.S.-Mexico border, they are also known as *ojos de agua* ("eyes of water"). By any name, they are natural rock basins that collect and hold rainwater and seasonal runoff during times of drought, and they have aided man in surviving and traversing the sere reaches of the Great Southwest since before recorded history. Water pockets can vary from a few inches deep and a body length in diameter to large, deep *tinajas* that hold thousands of gallons of water. You should know where these precious sources of water can be found along your route—as well as other natural water sources such as springs and creeks—and in what geological formation they're likely to be found. As further insurance when traveling the dry reaches of canyon country, you should also know where man-made water sources, such as wells and stock tanks, can be found. In trekking 60 miles down the length of the Kanab Creek canyon, for example, you'll need to locate Cedar Water Pocket in the Supai Formation in order to continue your canyon journey, as Major Powell's men had to do more than a century ago. If you scramble up 7,646-foot Shiva Temple in the Grand Canyon after a recent rain, you may be able to rely on the water pockets in the Esplanade Formation on Shiva Saddle to return to the North Rim, as the Anasazi did between A.D. 900 and 1100. And if you're following the Spanish Trail on foot toward the confluence of the Green and Colorado Rivers in Canyonlands National Park, you'll probably need to find the deep water pocket in the slickrock sandstone called *El Tenejal,* as the McComb Expedition had to do in 1859. Three other examples come immediately to mind. If you plan on traversing the 72-mile-long Tonto Trail, you'll find it advantageous to take your trip in the spring, both for the milder temperatures and to make use of seasonal runoff in the intervening canyons between the east and west ends of the Tonto Trail. If you're exploring the canyons of Tiburón Island in the Sea of Cortés, you'll need to find the ancestral spring that the Seri depended on and knew as *Pazj Hax*—what ethnographer William J. McGee's thirsty crew called Tinaja Anita in 1895. And if you're exploring the lofty heights of the Sierra del Carmen in the Big Bend frontier of Coahuila, you'll need to plan your route to make use of the unnamed spring in Barranca de Socavón to get back to the Río Grande–Río Bravo del Norte alive, as *candelilla* workers have done since 1911 when they first began smuggling burroloads of wax across the border.

Whether you're a novice or a veteran canyoneer, it's your responsibility to learn where dependable water sources are located along your proposed route of travel before you leave the trailhead. National parks in canyon country, such as the Grand Canyon, have a list of water sources, where they are located, and in what geological formation they can be found. This crucial information can be more difficult to come by if you plan on exploring canyons south of

Canyoneer Louise Teal cools off at Tinaja Anita on Tiburón Island, Sonora.

the U.S.-Mexico border. So if you don't know anyone who has first-hand knowledge and experience in the area, you'll have to do your homework and study the guidebooks and topographical maps. Hydrological and geological surveys are additional sources of valuable information, but if these monographs and surveys are your only sources, don't bet your life on that information being current and reliable without first checking with a local.

Plan your route so that it makes use of what you know are dependable water sources, but do not camp within a quarter mile of them, because wildlife—and in sparsely inhabited areas such as Mexico's Sierra Madre, people—also rely on them. You should also plan your route, if possible, to avoid making dry camps (without water).

Locating man-made water sources such as stock ponds and windmills is relatively easy if you study your topographical map and the horizon line. Incipient water sources can also be found if you know how to identify indicator plants such as cottonwood trees, maidenhair ferns, and other plants identified in the field guides listed in the Bibliography. Except possibly for what some call the Sonoran pronghorn antelope, all large mammals in the Great Southwest go to water; in the dry expanses of canyon country, their trails can also be good indicators, as are the flights of doves in the evening.

Water Purification. Wherever you get your water, always plan on purifying it. Many hikers now rely on water pumps (carry a bottle of water purification tablets in case it breaks down); I prefer the lightness and convenience of using iodine, and using clear, untreated water for the natural canyon aroma that comes from boiling fresh coffee grounds in the morning. Chlorine kills bacteria but not *Giardia*. If your only source of water is, say, the muddy Colorado River or the silt-laden Paria River, once you've refilled your water containers, you should let them stand overnight to allow the sediment to settle; once the sediment has settled, pour this clear water into another container and then purify it. If your water source is a bee-infested *tinaja*, leaf-covered water pocket, or scummy stock pond, put a bandanna over the mouth of your empty water bottle and strain the water through it before purifying it.

Water Caches. Throughout the decade I taught outdoor education in the Southwest, I led more than seventy multiday treks down the Grand Canyon's nonmaintained miner trails and routes. Most of my students were novice city slickers, and they varied in age from teenagers to retirees. To ensure their safety and comfort, I established the practice of caching food and water—but particularly water—approximately every 1,500 vertical feet we descended into the canyon along difficult rim-to-river routes such as Tanner Trail, Boucher Trail, and Hance Trail. At each cache, each student left a quart to a quart and a half of water and one meal that they could use on their daunting climb back out to the South rim. There was—and still is—little reason to carry $2^{1}/_{2}$ gallons (or 20 pounds) of water 10 or 12 miles down to the Colorado River if you're going to drink $1^{1}/_{2}$ gallons (or 12 pounds) of it on the climb back out to the rim. The same holds true for food. If your canyon route follows either a rim-to-river or a largely dry out-and-back route, you can make use of water and food caches. Animalproof your food by keeping it in tins or by tying your food bag up a piñon tree, and humanproof it by hiding it. If you can't hide it, clearly label your plastic water jugs with a heavy felt marker with a message along the lines of "Water cache. Please do not disturb. My life depends on it."

HAZARDS

The potential hazards and natural dangers awaiting the unwary in canyon country would keep them safely holed up in the IMAX Theater or Rain Forest Café until the urge passed—if they were cognizant. For those who do their homework, stay alert and attuned to the canyon environment, and use common sense, however, all but the unforeseen and acts of God can be avoided.

WEATHER
Flash floods. During 1997, summer monsoon weather in the Southwest created the most deadly flash-flood season in recent memory; thirteen canyoneers died after being swept away in two unrelated canyoneering incidents, and a third flash-flood tragedy claimed the

lives of eight Mexican citizens who drowned while crossing the U.S.-Mexico border between Douglas, Arizona, and Agua Prieta, Sonora. Let's take a closer look at the canyoneering tragedies and see what the common link was.

Against the advice of local Navajos, who warned the New Jersey tour group of the impending thunderstorm and extreme flash-flood danger, eleven canyoneers from France, England, Switzerland, and the United States were led back into the narrow, escape-proof corridor of Antelope Canyon by their tour guide. All but the guide perished when a 50-foot wall of water swept them to their death; some of the unrecovered bodies were believed to have been washed all the way out to Lake Powell. In a second, unrelated incident, three hikers were engulfed by a 5-foot wall of water several miles above Phantom Ranch when a flash flood roared down Phantom Creek; miraculously, one canyoneer survived a mile-long swim by using swift-water swimming techniques before managing to catch an eddy. In Havasu Creek, eighty other river runners and canyon day hikers were reportedly saved when a former track runner outran a flash flood, which was tumbling boulders the size of vans, and warned them to climb to high ground. Look at any one of these incidents, and each party was in the wrong place at the wrong time.

Stay out of dry washes and canyons during summer monsoons. As further insurance against flash-flood danger, my own rule of thumb is: Don't go near dry washes, narrows, deep canyons, or slot canyons if there are storm clouds brewing overhead or anywhere near the headwaters of the canyon or desert wash I want to explore.

Heat. You already have the common sense not to hike to the bottom of the Grand Canyon in June or July, but two thousand other hikers pay little heed to National Park Service warnings each summer day. It is a recipe for disaster that triggered more than 481 National Park Service search-and-rescue missions in 1996, which were often carried out at great personal risk to the searchers and rescuers. Stand on the edge of the South Rim near Kolbs Studio and you can watch columns of eager, unwary hikers and canyoneers march down the Bright Angel Trail into an oven hot enough to bake their brains and a skillet of cowboy muffins. Chances are that these hikers consider themselves to be in good shape on flat, cool ground, but if statistics are any indication, one of two general scenarios will play out for those who become canyon statistics: Their half-hour hike down the Bright Angel Trail turned into a day-long life-and-death struggle to reach the South Rim alive because they literally got sucked deeper and deeper into the great abyss by gravity, scenery, and euphoria. Or they were fit but were not acclimated to the heat, were not adequately rehydrated from the hike down to the Colorado River the day before, were more susceptible to the heat because they had closed the Phantom Ranch beer hall, didn't carry enough water to reach the South Rim, or didn't leave Bright Angel Campground early enough—5 A.M.—to beat the searing heat to the cooler elevation of the Tonto Formation. If they were struggling up the Bright Angel Trail and faltered from the heat, chances are they were lucky enough to become known as "dragouts," in the parlance of Grand Canyon mule skinners; or they had to be heli-vacced out at $1,000 or more per flight. If they were struggling up the lower third of the Tanner Trail or Nankoweap Trail and they faltered from the heat without adequate water and didn't immediately go back to the river or creek to rehydrate and recover, chances are they became victims.

Symptoms of dehydration include thirst, dizziness, nausea, and loss of motor coordination and mental drive. Treatment includes cooling down the victim by getting him or her into the shade, applying moist cloths to the forehead and the carotid arteries of the neck, and rehydrating with adequate water. *Warning:* Unless you're a fit canyoneering veteran who is well acclimated to heavy and prolonged physical exertion in extreme heat, stay the hell out of the desert canyon country during the summer. Avoid beer, wine, and hard liquor for several nights before you trek, because alcohol will make you more susceptible to the heat. Be well hydrated before your trek; clear urine is a good indicator. And plan on carrying and drinking a minimum of 2 gallons of water or more each day; the gallon-a-day rule of thumb is poppycock. My own fluid requirement formula is to carry—or be able to resupply from a personal cache or a reliable natural water source—a gallon of water for every 10 linear miles I plan to trek; I allow an additional quart or more of water—depending on how much weight I'm carrying—for each 1,000 vertical feet I need to climb. And if by chance I need to climb out of the bottom of the Grand Canyon during extreme heat—or the equivalent, such as the Barranca del Cobre—I add a third gallon of water to my requirement allotment.

Let me give you two examples: To stay well hydrated during a four-day bighorn sheep count in the Barry M. Goldwater Range during 115° June heat, I drank 2$\frac{1}{2}$ to 3 gallons of water a day; I ran 10 miles each day at first light and holed up in the shade of a cave the remaining twenty-two hours each day. On another occasion, before embarking on a steep, grueling search of the South Kaibab Trail for a lost foreign diplomat one blistering June day, I prehydrated the hour before at Phantom Ranch by drinking a gallon and a half of water; I carried another gallon and a half of water in my pack, which I consumed before reaching the South Rim three and a half hours later.

Lightning and Wind. Lightning reportedly kills an average of ninety-six Americans each year. It can strike anywhere during summer monsoon weather, as two German tourists discovered while standing at a South Rim vista staring into the Grand Canyon.

When it comes to lightning storms, I have several rules of thumb. The most effective is to stay out of them. But if for some reason I've misjudged the weather, there are three rules of thumb for Plan B: (1) Don't stand on the high ground (such as a canyon rim), (2) don't be the high ground (while walking across flat terrain such as a broad terrace), and (3) don't sit beneath the high ground (such as a tree). If possible, seek the safety of natural shelters such as the overhang of a ledge or a boulder, but remember, when it comes to caves, lightning can conduct down rain-slickened cracks. Sit on your foam pad and avoid metal objects such as your pack frame. During high winds, avoid exposed scrambling and traversing narrow ledges, because high winds can literally blow you off precipitous perches. During summer months, hot winds can wick away precious moisture from your body and enhance dehydration, and in cooler temperatures, they can cause hypothermia—a dangerous lowering of the body's inner core temperature—if you're not adequately clothed or can't come in out of the wind.

RIVER AND CREEK CROSSINGS

Cross-canyon routes that involve river crossings can be far more dangerous in the Grand Canyon than in someplace like the border canyons of Big Bend, because the Colorado River is much swifter, larger, and colder than the Río Grande–Río Bravo del Norte, averaging a bone-numbing 45° to 55° Fahrenheit. Hitching a ride across the river with river runners is the safest bet. If, however, your route necessitates a river crossing and does not coincide with river-running season, you need to pack in and wear a Sterns Type III life preserver with a collar and use a one-man military survival raft (or a sturdy commercial equivalent). River crossings should be made in absolutely calm weather, a mile below rapids, eddies, whirlpools, and other turbulent water. If you plan to explore a national park canyon, check with the backcountry ranger's office for river-crossing permits, the safest areas to cross, and other pertinent up-to-date information.

Creek crossings are another matter: They can vary from the relatively easy fords of Aravaipa Creek to the treacherous narrows of

A Mexican vaquero *hitches a ride with Outward Bound canoeists across the Río Bravo del Norte (above and opposite) to look for a stray calf in the border canyons of Big Bend National Park, Texas.*

Wreck at Disaster Falls
BOGERT; J. W. POWELL

Tapeats Creek. Avoid deep creek crossings during spring runoff or summer monsoon season, when flash floods present a deadly hazard. If a creek looks too swift and deep to cross, don't chance it. You can check the depth and strength of the current by using a stick such as an agave stalk; if it is more than thigh deep and the current looks like it's strong enough to knock you down, go back or go around if you have any doubts about your ability to negotiate the creek crossing safely. Use a walking stick for balance, face upstream against the current, and cross in the calmest, shallowest, and most benign stretches; carry your pack overhead in case you slip and need to toss it before lunging for the other side.

Swift-Water Swimming. Never wear your pack during river crossings. If you've misjudged your crossing point and your one-man raft capsizes and lurches beyond reach, lay back in your life vest with your knees bent and your feet pointed downstream to push off boulders, and paddle with your arms and hands at your sides until you've negotiated the rapid and can swim to shore.

Quicksand. Try as I might, I could not sink more than thigh deep in Paria Canyon's quicksand. If there is a pool of quicksand in canyon country that will suck you helplessly down to the bottom, I have not found it. If you have, and you insist on toying with it, have a cowboy and a good cutting horse on standby to drag your bawling hide out with a rope.

ROCKFALL AND CLIFF FALLS

In 1994, snowmelt triggered a rock slide that sounded "like a bomb in a bunkhouse," injuring four river runners camped on the south shore of the Colorado River in the Grand Canyon. I've found such incidents to be a rarity in canyon country, mainly because natural rockfall generally occurs during snowmelt and summer monsoons. Canyoneers are far more likely to knock stones and boulders down on one another than they are to hear and witness this relatively rare phenomenon. There are some simple rules of thumb: On steep and precipitous terrain, watch where you place your feet, don't stand on a loose rock or hollow-sounding boulder that you know is going to crush your companions below, and stay out of one another's fall lines while descending, scrambling, and pulling down the rappel rope. The same rules apply to falling off cliffs: Don't climb around the edges of precipitous ledges and cliffs unroped. If an inclined pitch looks dicey to you, don't climb it unroped, because chances are you won't be able to safely down-climb or reverse your moves without falling.

FLORA AND FAUNA

Poisonous Plants. The witches' brew of the poisonous plants waiting to infect you in canyon country runs the gamut from poison ivy to sacred datura and wild mushrooms. If you don't already know how to identify the poisonous plants of canyon country, visit the local botanical gardens or study the illustrated field guides listed in the Bibliography. The most worrisome plant for canyoneers, perhaps, is poison ivy; know this plant and how to avoid it. New over-the-counter treatments claim to offer protection from poison ivy before contact, but I refuse to experiment on myself. Finally, don't eat any plants you didn't bring with you.

Cactus. Cactus thorns, spines, and tiny needles called glochids can be troublesome. Be careful what you grab and where you place your feet and legs. If you can't stay out of the cholla patch, have two items ready: a comb to remove the cactus ball or spine, and tweezers to remove the needles and glochids.

Much hot air has been written about using cactus as a reliable water source in an emergency. If you do nothing but sit still in 110° summer shade for twenty-four hours, your body will use a minimum of a gallon to a gallon and a half of water, depending on your body weight. Think of the cactus myth this way: When was the last time you ate an entire watermelon to stay alive, day in and day out? Try two of them. Now imagine that you're on the verge of heat-stroke, you're dizzy, and you're nauseous. Can you cut, skin, and suck a gallon of moisture out of a hot, withered-looking prickly pear cactus that isn't anywhere near as palatable as an ice-cold watermelon? No. Can you uproot and pry open a barrel cactus covered with fishhook spines and pound down even a single quart of hot, bitter pulp without vomiting it all over yourself and your companions? I doubt it. Assuming that you know how to get into a teddy bear cholla cactus (and I won't tell you how to do it), can you gather, peel, and eat a gallon and a half of pulp, day after day? I don't think so. I've tried them all in dire situations, while trekking in extreme desert conditions, and I couldn't. More power to you if you can. If, however, you happen to be in cactus country when fruit such as a prickly pear, saguaro, and pitaya are ripe for plucking, your odds are better. But you still have to remove the clusters of tiny spines to eat them. Even as delectable as cactus fruit appears to be, don't count on being able to eat enough to continue moving from Point A to Point B; unless you are a full-blooded Seri still living in one of the harshest deserts ever inhabited by man, you will need to drink water—lots of it. If you plan on canyoneering in the Great Southwest during the summertime, you should plan on drinking a minimum of 2 to 3 gallons of water a day. Don't lose sight of that fact or your need to regularly supply from dependable water sources, and don't leave your last dependable water source without enough water to return to it if your next water source comes up dry.

Poisonous Reptiles, Spiders, and Insects. There are two expressions, among many, to live or die by in Arizona: "If it doesn't stick or scratch you, it can bite you," and "Don't put your hands or feet where you can't see." The reason is simple. There is a diverse array of rattlesnakes you can encounter in canyon country, and the toxins they can inject range from the hemotoxin of the western diamondback to the neurotoxin of the Mojave rattlesnake. Suggested field treatments are controversial and vary widely; they include the dangerous cut-and-suck method; ligature-cryotherapy, hydrocortisone injections, antivenin, and do nothing but get the victim to help. I'm from the stay-calm, wait and see school; if the pit viper has envenomated (and it's been estimated that rattlesnakes do so about 50 percent of the time), I would use the small vacuum pump (called The Extractor, from Sawyer's First Aid Kit) I carry with me in snake country to extract the toxin, then go for help (or if I've been bitten, send someone else for help). According to the Phoenix, Arizona–based Desert Alpine Reserve Emergency Services group: "Of about six thousand persons bitten by poisonous snakes in the United States each year, only about twelve die and many of the survivors have no first aid treatment whatsoever." If poisonous reptiles, spiders, scorpions, and insects don't live in your backyard, learn how to identify them by studying illustrated field guides.

Other poisonous reptiles include the Gila monster and its cousin the Mexican beaded lizard. Unless you're doing something foolish, like showing your friends what a wizened desert rat you are, your chances of being bitten by one of these sluggish, colorful lizards are remote. Slender scorpions are more common and can be detected in your campsite by using a black light at night or by shaking out your boots and ground cloth the next morning. Spiders range from the black widow to the brown recluse. Allergic reactions to bee stings are reported to be of greater concern, so don't rile them up by trying to steal their honey. The most common and painful bite or sting I've seen among canyoneers—and experienced myself, including a slender scorpion sting—is a red ant bite. Carry a sting applicator that detoxifies the bite with ammonia. And before you head out to canyon country, go back to the library and do your homework. Know how to identify poisonous reptiles, spiders, and insects; their habits and habitat; how to avoid them; and the best treatment.

GEAR CHECKLIST

I'm from the low-tech school—what I used to chide my elders as being the old school. By either name, I prefer to rely on knowledge, experience, conditioning, acclimatization, and mental preparedness rather than relying on high-tech gear. Listed here are the bare-bones items I've used to travel safely through canyon country for the last two decades. You can add to this list as you desire.

FEET
- Running shoes or lightweight hiking boots
- Wool socks
- Moleskin

LOWER EXTREMITIES
- Shorts
- Long pants for brush
- Wool or polypropylene long johns for cold, damp conditions

UPPER EXTREMITIES
- Cotton T-shirt
- Wool or polypropylene long-sleeved shirt for cold, damp conditions
- Jacket
- Rain gear, if weather dictates

HEAD AND NECK
- Bandannas for neck and head
- Ball cap
- Wool watch cap for night and cold, damp conditions

HANDS
- Wool gloves if cold, damp conditions dictate

PACK

- Day pack or internal-framed overnight pack
- Water bottles: 1-gallon plastic jug (full), two 1-quart bottles (full), and, if needed for resupply, one to 3 empty 1-gallon plastic jugs
- Water purification: iodine tablets, bandanna
- Pocketknife
- Cooking: white gas stove, metal cook pan, cup, spoon, food, coffee
- Orientation: compass, topographical maps in Ziploc bag, pencil
- First-aid kit: aspirin, surgical adhesive tape, bandannas, venom extractor
- Emergencies: signal mirror, matches in waterproof container
- Tent, if no known natural shelters along travel route, and if weather dictates

FLOTATION (IF ROUTE DICTATES)

- One-man military surplus survival raft
- U.S. Diver's inflatable life vest
- Dry bag, with shoulder straps

RAPPEL GEAR (IF ROUTE DICTATES)

- 150-foot perlon rope
- Helmet
- 12 carabiners (2 that are locking)
- 4 1 x 3-inch-diameter tubular webbing nylon slings
- $1/4$-inch gold-line Prusik knot for self-belay
- Set of Jumars and stirrups (if route dictates)

IN VEHICLE

- Extra food and 5 gallons extra water
- Shovel
- Major first-aid kit and manual *Medicine for Mountaineering*
- Flares

WATER REQUIREMENT CHARTS

(from *The Physiology of Man in the Desert* by Adolph & Associates)

A. Number of Days Expected Survival in Desert, No Walking at All:

Available water per man, U.S. quarts	0	1	2	4	10	20
Max. daily shade temp. °F	**Days of expected survival**					
120°	2	2	2	2.5	3	4.5
110°	3	3	3.5	4	5	7
100°	5	5.5	6	7	9.5	13.5
90°	7	8	9	10.5	15	23
80°	9	10	11	13	19	29
70°	10	11	12	14	20.5	32
60°	10	11	12	14	21	32
50°	10	11	12	14.5	21	32

B. Number of Days of Expected Survival in Desert, Walking at Night Until Exhausted and Resting Thereafter:

Available water per man, U.S. quarts	0	1	2	4	10	20
Max. daily shade temp. °F	**Days of expected survival**					
120°	1	2	2	2.5	3	–
110°	1	2	2.5	3	3.5	–
100°	3	3.5	3.5	4.5	5.5	–
90°	5	5.5	5.5	6.5	8	–
80°	7	7.5	8	9.5	11.5	–
70°	7.5	8	9	10.5	13.5	–
60°	8	8.5	9	11	14	–
50°	8	8.5	9	11	14	–

BIBLIOGRAPHY

GENERAL

Abbey, Edward. *Desert Solitaire.* New York: Ballantine, 1968.

———. *The Hidden Canyon: A River Journey.* Introduction by Martin Litton. Photographs by John Blaustein. New York: Penguin Books, 1977.

———. *Slickrock: Endangered Canyons of the Southwest.* Photographs by Philip Hyde. Layton, UT: Peregrine Smith Books, 1987.

Annerino, John. *High Risk Photography: The Adventure Behind the Image.* Photographs by the author. Helena, MT: American & World Geographic, 1991.

———. *Canyons of the Southwest: A Tour of the Great Canyon Country from Colorado to Northern Mexico.* Photographs by the author. San Francisco: Sierra Club Books, 1993.

———. *The Wild Country of Mexico: La tierra salvaje de México.* Photographs by the author. San Francisco: Sierra Club Books, 1994 (bilingual).

———. *People of Legend: Native Americans of the Southwest.* Photographs by the author. San Francisco: Sierra Club Books, 1996.

———. *Running Wild: An Extraordinary Adventure of the Human Spirit.* Photographs by Christine Keith. New York: Thunder's Mouth Press, 1998.

Beer, Bill. *We Swam the Grand Canyon.* Seattle: Mountaineers, 1998.

Bennett, Wendall C., and Robert M. Zingg. *The Tarahumara: An Indian Tribe of Northwest Mexico.* Photographs by Fr. Luis G. Verplancken, S.J. Glorieta, NM: Río Grande Press, 1976.

Bolton, Herbert Eugene, ed. *Spanish Exploration in the Southwest. 1542–1706.* New York: Charles Scribner's Sons, 1916.

————, trans. and ed. *Pageant in the Wilderness: The Story of The Escalante Expedition to the Interior Basin, 1776.* Salt Lake City: Utah State Historical Society, 1950.

Bones, Jim. *Río Grande: Mountains to the Sea.* Photographs by the author. Austin: Texas Monthly Press, 1985.

Bowden, Charles. *The Secret Forest.* Photographs by Jack Dykinga. Albuquerque: University of New Mexico Press, 1993.

————. *Stone Canyons of the Colorado Plateau.* Photographs by Jack Dykinga. New York: Harry N. Abrams, 1996.

Brooks, Juanita, and Robert Glass Cleland. *A Mormon Chronicle: The Diaries of John D. Lee, 1848–1876.* San Marino, CA: Huntington Library, 1955.

Brower, David Ross. *The Place No One Knew: Glen Canyon on the Colorado.* Photographs by Eliot Porter. Layton, UT: Peregrine Smith Books, 1988.

Brown, David E. *The Wolf in the Southwest: The Making of an Endangered Species.* Tucson: University of Arizona Press, 1983.

Carmony, Neil B. *Onza! The Hunt for a Legendary Cat.* Silver City, NM: High Lonesome Books, 1995.

Carmony, Neil B., and David E. Brown, eds. *Tales from Tiburon: An Anthology of Adventures in Seriland.* Phoenix: Southwest Natural History Association, 1983.

————. *The Wilderness of the Southwest: Charles Sheldon's Quest for Desert Bighorn and Adventures with the Havasupai and Seri Indians.* Photographs by Charles Sheldon and E. A. Goldman. Salt Lake City: University of Utah Press, 1993.

Collins, Robert O., and Roderick Nash. *The Big Drops: Ten Legendary Rapids of the American West.* Boulder, CO: Johnson Books, 1989.

Coues, Elliott, trans. and ed. *On the Trail of the Spanish Pioneer: The Diary and Itinerary of Francisco Garcés, 1775–1776.* 2 vols. New York: Francis P. Harper, 1900.

Crampton, C. Gregory: *Standing Up Country: The Canyonlands of Utah and Arizona.* Photographs by others. New York: Alfred A. Knopf and University of Utah Press, 1964.

————. *Land of Living Rock: The Grand Canyon and the High Plateaus: Arizona, Utah, and Nevada.* Photographs by C. Gregory Crampton and others. New York: Alfred A. Knopf, 1972.

Cudahy, John. *Mañanaland: Adventuring with Camera and Rifle Through California and Mexico.* New York: Duffield, 1928.

Curtis, Edward Sheriff. *The North American Indian: Being a Series of Volumes Picturing and Describing the Indians of the United States and Alaska.* Photographs by the author. Cambridge, MA: University Press, 1907–1930.

D'Azevedo, Warren L., ed. *Handbook of North American Indians.* Vol. 11, *Great Basin.* Washington, DC: Smithsonian Institution, 1986.

Dawson, Thomas F. *First Through the Grand Canyon.* U.S. Senate, 1st Session, Exec. Doc. 42, Res. No. 79, June 4, 1917.

Dellenbaugh, Frederick S. *Romance of the Colorado River.* New York: G. P. Putnam's Sons, 1906.

———. *A Canyon Voyage: The Narrative of the Second Powell Expedition down the Green-Colorado River from Wyoming, and the Explorations on Land, in the Years 1871 and 1872.* New Haven, CT: Yale University Press, 1926.

Doolittle, Jerome. *Canyons and Mesas.* Photographs by Wolf Von Dem Bussche. The American Wilderness series. New York: Time-Life Books, 1974.

Dutton, Clarence Edward. *Tertiary History of the Grand Canyon, with Atlas.* Department of Interior Monographs of the U.S. Geological Survey, Vol. 2. Washington, DC: U.S. Government Printing Office, 1882.

Emory, William H. *Report on the United States and Mexico Boundary Survey.* Vol. 1. Washington, DC: Cornelius Wendell, 1857.

Fisher, Richard D. *National Parks of Northern Mexico.* Photographs by the author. Tucson: Sunracer Publications, 1994.

———. *Earth's Mystical Grand Canyons.* Photographs by the author. Tucson: Sunracer Publications, 1995.

Fletcher, Colin. *The Man Who Walked Through Time.* New York: Alfred A. Knopf, 1968.

Fontana, Bernard L. *Tarahumara: Where Night Is Day of the Moon.* Photographs by John Paul Schaefer. Tucson: University of Arizona Press, 1997.

Gregory, Herbert Ernest, and Robert C. Moore. *The Kaiparowits Region: A Geographic and Geologic Reconnaissance of Parts of Utah and Arizona.* Washington, DC: U.S. Government Printing Office, 1931.

"Guide Locates Missing Pilot: Floating on Log Raft." *Arizona Daily Star* (Tucson), August 2, 1959, 2.

Hayden, F. V. *Annual Report of the United States Geological and Geographical Survey of the Territories Embracing Colorado and Parts of Adjacent Territories: Being a Report of Progress of the Exploration for the Year 1874.* Washington, DC: U.S. Government Printing Office, 1876.

Heald, Weldon F. "How deep are those Mexican barrancas?" Photographs by the author. *Pacific Discovery* 11, no. 5 (Sept.–Oct. 1958): 22–27.

Horgan, Paul. *Great River: The Río Grande in North American History.* 2 vols. New York: Rinehart & Co., 1954.

Hughes, J. Donald. *The Story of Man at the Grand Canyon.* Grand Canyon, AZ: Grand Canyon Natural History Association, 1967.

Ives, Joseph Christmas. *Report upon the Colorado River of the West: Explored in 1857 and 1858.* Washington, DC: U.S. Government Printing Office, 1861.

Jackson, Donald Dale, and Peter Wood. *The Sierra Madre.* Photographs by Dan Budnick. The American Wilderness series. Alexandria, VA: Time-Life Books, 1975.

James, George Wharton. *In and Around the Grand Canyon.* Boston: Little, Brown, 1900.

———. *The Grand Canyon of Arizona: How to See It.* Boston: Little, Brown, 1910.

Johnson, William Weber. *Baja California.* Photographs by Jan Maisel. The American Wilderness series. New York: Time-Life Books, 1972.

Kolb, Emery. *Through the Grand Canyon from Wyoming to Mexico.* Foreword by Owen Wister. Photographs by Emery and Ellsworth Kolb. New York: Macmillan, 1920.

Lavender, David Seibert. *Colorado River Country.* New York: E. P. Dutton, 1982.

———. *River Runners of the Grand Canyon.* Grand Canyon, AZ: Grand Canyon Natural History Association, 1985.

Leavengood, Betty. *Grand Canyon Women: Lives Shaped by Landscape.* Boulder, CO: Pruett Publishing, 1999.

Lingenfelter, Richard E. *First Through the Grand Canyon*. Los Angeles: Glen Dawson, 1958.

Lobeck, A. K. *Physiographic Provinces of North America* (map). New York: Columbia University/Geographic Press, 1948.

———. *Physiographic Diagram of North America*. Maplewood, NJ: Hamond/Geographic Press, 1950.

Lumholtz, Carl. *Unknown Mexico: A Record of Five Years' Exploration Among the Tribes of the Western Sierra Madre; in the Tierra Caliente of Tepic and Jalisco; and Among the Tarascos of Michoacán*. Vols. 1 and 2. Photographs by the author. New York: Charles Scribner's Sons, 1902.

———. *Los Indios del Noroeste, 1890–1898*. Photographs by the author. México, DF: INI-FONOPAS, 1982.

———. *Montañas, duendes, adivinos. . . .* Prólogo by Jesus Jáuregui. Texto by Mario R. Vázquez. Photographs by the author. México, DF: Instituto Nacional Indigenista, 1996.

Lummis, Charles Fletcher. *Mesa, Cañon, and Pueblo*. New York: Appleton-Century, 1938.

Matthiessen, Peter. *Indian Country*. New York: Penguin Books, 1992.

Merriam, C. Hart. "Results of a Biological Survey of the San Francisco Mountain Region and Desert of the Little Colorado, Arizona." North American Fauna, No. 3. (Sept. 11). U.S. Department of Agriculture, Division of Ornithology and Mammalogy. Washington, DC: U.S. Government Printing Office, 1890.

Ortiz, Alfonso, ed. *Handbook of North American Indians*. Vol. 9, *Southwest*. Washington, DC: Smithsonian Institution, 1979.

———. *Handbook of North American Indians*. Vol. 10, *Southwest*. Washington, DC: Smithsonian Institution, 1983.

Page, Jake. *Hopi*. Photographs by Susanne Page. New York: Harry N. Abrams, 1982.

———. *Navajo*. Photographs by Susanne Page. New York: Harry N. Abrams, 1995.

Peattie, Roderick, and Weldon F. Heald, eds. *The Inverted Mountains: Canyons of the West*. New York: Vanguard Press, 1948.

Powell, John Wesley. *Explorations of the Colorado River of the West and Its Tributaries: Explored in 1869, 1870, 1871, and 1872*. Washington, DC: U.S. Government Printing Office, 1875.

————. *An Overland Trip to the Grand Cañon.* Palmer Lake, CO: Filter Lake Press, 1974.

Reisner, Marc. *Cadillac Desert: The American West and Its Disappearing Water.* New York: Viking Penguin, 1986.

"Rock slide rumbles through campsite in Grand Canyon, hurting 4 rafters." *Arizona Daily Star* (Tucson), October 18, 1994, 1.

Rusho, W. L. *Everett Reuss: A Vagabond for Beauty.* Introduction by John Nichols. Afterword by Edward Abbey. Salt Lake City: Peregrine Smith Books, 1983.

Rusho, W. L., and C. Gregory Crampton. *Desert River Crossing: Historic Lees Ferry on the Colorado River.* Salt Lake City: Peregrine Smith, 1975.

Sadler, Christa, et al. *There's This River: Grand Canyon Boatmen Stories.* Flagstaff, AZ: Red Lake Books, 1994.

Shaffer, Mark. "Missing in Canyon Flashflood: No warning of downpour on plateau, survivor says." *The Arizona Republic* (Phoenix), September 3, 1997, B-1.

Shaffer, Mark, and Steve Yozwiak. "11 Hikers Killed in Flash Flood: Tragedy in Antelope Canyon." *The Arizona Republic* (Phoenix) August 14, 1997, 1.

Shephard, Grant. *The Silver Magnet: Fifty Years in a Mexican Silver Mine.* New York: E. P. Dutton, 1938.

Shultheis, Rob. *The Hidden West: Journeys in the American Outback.* San Francisco: North Point Press, 1983.

Smith, Melvin T. *The Colorado River: Its History in the Lower Canyons Area.* Provo, UT: Brigham Young University, 1972.

Smithers, Wilfred Dudley. *Chronicles of the Big Bend: A Photographic Memoir of Life on the Border.* Photographs by the author. Austin, TX: Madrona Press, 1976.

Steiger, Lew. "Kenton Grua." *Boatman's Quarterly Review, The Journal of Grand Canyon River Guides, Inc.* 11, no. 1 (winter 1997–98): 36–47.

Sterling, Keir B. *Last of the Naturalists: The Career of C. Hart Merriam.* New York: Arno Press, 1974.

Stoffle, Richard W., et al. *Piapaxa 'Uipi (Big River Canyon).* Bureau of Applied Research in Anthropology. Tucson: University of Arizona Press, 1994.

Stone, Julius. *Canyon Country: The Romance of a Drop of Water and a Grain of Sand.* New York: G. P. Putnam's Sons, 1932.

Teal, Louise. *Breaking into the Current: Boatwomen of the Grand Canyon.* Tucson: University of Arizona Press, 1994.

Traven, B. *The Treasure of the Sierra Madre.* New York: Alfred A. Knopf, 1935.

Tyler, Ronald C. *The Big Bend: A History of the Last Texas Frontier.* Washington, DC: U.S. Department of the Interior, 1975.

Wallace, Robert. *The Grand Canyon.* Photographs by Ernst Haas. The American Wilderness series. New York: Time-Life Books, 1972.

Yetman, David. *Sonora: An Intimate Geography.* Albuquerque: University of New Mexico Press, 1996.

Yozwiak, Steve. "Nature Often Wins in Park: Grand Canyon extremely unforgiving." *The Arizona Republic* (Phoenix), August 7, 1996, 1.

———. "Mad Dash Alerts Dozens to Havasu Creek Danger." *The Arizona Republic* (Phoenix), August 18, 1997, 1.

NATURAL HISTORY, WILDERNESS TRAVEL, AND RIVER GUIDES

Annerino, John. *Hiking the Grand Canyon.* San Francisco: Sierra Club Books, 1986. Revised edition 1993, with fold-out map by the author, drawn by Hilda Chen.

———. *Adventuring in Arizona.* San Francisco: Sierra Club Books, 1991. Revised edition 1996.

Aulbach, Louis F., and Joe Butler. *The Lower Canyons of the Río Grande: La Linda to Dryden Crossing, Maps and Notes for River Runners.* Houston: Wilderness Area Map Service, 1993.

Barnes, Fran A. *Canyon Country Hiking and Natural History.* Salt Lake City: Wasatch Publishers, 1977.

Barnes, William C. *Arizona Place Names.* Foreword by Bernard L. Fontana. Tucson: University of Arizona Press, 1988.

Belknap, Buzz. *Canyonlands River Guide: Westwater, Lake Powell, Canyonlands National Park.* Boulder City, NV: Westwater Books, 1974.

Belknap, William "Buzz" III. *Grand Canyon River Guide.* Boulder City, NV: Westwater Books, 1969.

Belknap, Buzz, and Laura Evans. *Dinosaur River Guide: Flaming Gorge, Dinosaur National Monument.* Boulder City, NV: Westwater Books, 1973.

———. *Desolation River Guide: Green River Wilderness.* Boulder City, NV: Westwater Books, 1974.

Bjornstad, Eric. *Desert Rock.* Denver: Chockstone Press, 1988.

Brian, Nancy. *River to Rim: A Guide to Place Names Along the Colorado River in Grand Canyon, from Lake Powell to Lake Mead.* Flagstaff, AZ: Earthquest Press, 1992.

Brown, David E. *Biotic Communities: Southwestern United States and Northwestern Mexico.* Salt Lake City: University of Utah Press, 1994.

Butchart, Harvey. *Grand Canyon Treks: A Guide to Inner Canyon Routes.* Glendale, CA: La Siesta Press, 1970.

———. *Grand Canyon Treks II.* Glendale, CA: La Siesta Press, 1975.

———. *Grand Canyon Treks III.* Glendale, CA: La Siesta Press, 1984.

Canfield, Delos Lincoln. *The University of Chicago Spanish Dictionary.* Chicago: University of Chicago, 1987.

Fisher, Richard D., with Kit Williams. *Mexico's Copper Canyon.* Photographs by Richard D. Fisher. Tucson: Sunracer Publications, 1996.

Hamblin, W. Kenneth, and Joseph P. Murphy. *Grand Canyon Perspectives: A Guide to the Canyon's Scenery by Means of Interpretive Panoramas.* Provo, UT: Brigham Young University, 1969.

Hansen, Wallace R. *The Black Canyon of the Gunnison: In Depth.* Tucson: Southwest Parks and Monuments Association, 1987.

Jones, Stan. *Boating and Exploring Map: Lake Powell and Its Canyons.* Page, AZ: Sun Country Publications, 1980.

Kelsey, Michael R. *Canyon Hiking Guide to the Colorado Plateau.* Provo, UT: Kelsey Publishing, 1986.

———. *Hiking and Exploring the Paria River.* Provo, UT: Kelsey Publishing, 1987.

Kulander, Charles. *West Mexico. from Sea to Sierra: A Traveler's Handbook to the Baja Peninsula and Mexico's West Coast.* Ramona, CA: La Paz Publishing, 1992.

Lambrechtse, Rudi. *Hiking the Escalante.* Salt Lake City: Wasatch Publishers, 1985.

Loughman, Michael. *Learning to Rock Climb.* San Francisco: Sierra Club Books, 1981.

Lowe, Charles H. *Arizona's Natural Environment: Landscapes and Habitats.* Tucson: University of Arizona Press, 1964.

MacInnes, Hamish. *International Mountain Rescue Handbook.* New York: Charles Scribner's Sons, 1972.

MacMahon, James A. *Deserts.* Audubon Society Nature Guide. New York: Alfred A. Knopf, 1985.

Mitchell, Rodger. *Grand Canyon Jeep Trails.* Glendale, CA: La Siesta Press, 1977.

National Park Service. *Big Bend: Floating the Río Grande.* Washington, DC: National Park Service, U.S. Department of the Interior, 1983.

O'Rourke, P. J. *Holidays in Hell.* New York: Vintage Departures, 1992.

Pearson, John, ed. *River Guide to the Río Grande: General Information.* Big Bend, TX: Big Bend Natural History Association, 1982.

———. *River Guide 1 to the Río Grande: Colorado Canyon Through Santa Elena Canyon.* Big Bend, TX: Big Bend Natural History Association, 1982, revised edition 1992.

———. *River Guide 2 to the Río Grande: Mariscal Canyon Through Boquillas Canyon.* Big Bend, TX: Big Bend Natural History Association, 1982, revised edition 1989.

Peters, Ed, ed. *Mountaineering: The Freedom of the Hills.* 4th ed. Seattle: The Mountaineers, 1982.

Peterson, Walt. *The Baja Adventure Book.* Berkeley, CA: Wilderness Press, 1987.

Robbins, Royal. *Basic Rockcraft.* Glendale, CA: La Siesta Press, 1971.

———. *Advanced Rockcraft.* Glendale, CA: La Siesta Press, 1973.

Robinson, John W. *Camping and Climbing in Baja.* Glendale, CA: La Siesta Press, 1967.

Scott, Doug. *Big Wall Climbing.* New York: Oxford University Press, 1974.

Spamer, Earle E., ed. *Bibliography of the Grand Canyon and the Lower Colorado River, 1540–1980.* Grand Canyon, AZ: Grand Canyon Natural History Association, 1981.

Stevens, Larry. *The Colorado River in Grand Canyon: A Comprehensive Guide to Its Human and Natural History.* Flagstaff, AZ: Red Lake Books, 1983.

Stokes, Wm. Lee. *Scenes of the Plateau Lands and How They Came to Be.* Sketches by the author. Salt Lake City: Starstone Publishing, 1969.

Thybony, Scott. *A Guide to Hiking the Inner Canyon.* Grand Canyon, AZ: Grand Canyon Natural History Association, 1980.

United States Marine Corps. *Marine Combat Water Survival.* FMFRP 0-13, PNC 140 000 13000 Washington, DC: U.S. Marine Corps, 1991.

Waur, Roland H. *Hiker's Guide to the Developed Trails and Primitive Routes, Big Bend National Park.* Big Bend, TX: Big Bend Natural History Association, 1971.

Wheelock, Walt. *Ropes, Knots, and Slings for Climbers.* Glendale, CA: La Siesta Press, 1960. Revised edition 1982, Royal Robbins.

Whitney, Stephen. *Western Forests.* Audubon Society Nature Guide. New York: Alfred A. Knopf, 1985.

Wilkerson, James A., M.D., ed. *Medicine for Mountaineering.* 2d ed. Seattle: The Mountaineers, 1975.

ABOUT THE AUTHOR

Acclaimed author and photojournalist John Annerino was born on the edge of the desert and cut his teeth in the heart of the American West. The consummate Arizona native, he has been working in the frontier of Old Mexico and the American West for the last two decades, documenting its natural beauty, its indigenous people, and its political upheaval. Annerino is represented by the Liaison International picture agency in New York and Paris, and his credits include *Life, Time, Newsweek,* the *New York Times,* and *Scientific American,* among many other prestigious publications worldwide. He is the author of nine other books, including five photo-essays on this mythic region and the spirited individualists and Native people who've lived here since the time of legend.

Annerino has spent most of his life exploring the American West and the frontier of Old Mexico as a photojournalist, wilderness runner, and adventurer. He has been described as a scholar of southwestern history, and his knowledge of this mythical terrain, and the Native Americans who still inhabit it, is extensive. Among his many explorations by foot, raft, and rope, he has worked as a white-water boatman and paddle captain on the Green, Yampa, Colorado, and Upper Salt Rivers; a wilderness survival and climbing instructor in Arizona; and a forest firefighter and heli-vac crew boss in Alaska, British Columbia, and Washington. He has made half a dozen first ascents of Grand Canyon temples, led more than seventy trips into the inner Canyon as a teacher and guide, and run the length of the Grand Canyon by three different routes between 1980 and 1982 to prove his Native American travel theories. In 1988, Annerino ran 750 miles of daunting Arizona wilderness from Mexico to Utah as a way of further exploring the ancient ways of Native American routes and running. And in 1989, he led the first modern, unsupported traverse of the deadly Camino del Diablo on foot in midsummer. To date, John Annerino has explored more than fifty-thousand recorded miles of primitive trails and Native American routes by running, trekking, hiking, and canyoneering.

INDEX